Communication and the small group

THE BOBBS-MERRILL SERIES IN *Speech Communication*

RUSSEL R. WINDES, *Editor*

Queens College of the City University of New York

GERALD M. PHILLIPS

The Pennsylvania State University

Communication and the small group

The Bobbs-Merrill Company, Inc.
A SUBSIDIARY OF HOWARD W. SAMS & CO., INC.
PUBLISHERS   INDIANAPOLIS   NEW YORK   KANSAS CITY

Copyright © 1966 by The Bobbs-Merrill Company, Inc.
Printed in the United States of America
Library of Congress Catalog Card Number: 66-15381
First Printing

Preface

The writer wishes to express his gratitude to Mary Arnold, Don Huf-
hines, and Lou Pansky of the Western Branch, American Public
Health Association, for permitting me to experiment with both standard agenda and PERT; to my former colleague, Dr. Eugene Erickson,
for his perennial instruction in the sociology of small groups; and to
my present colleagues, Dr. Robert T. Oliver and Dr. Theodore Grove,
for careful reading of the manuscript and excellent suggestions for
revision. Appreciation is also extended to Dr. Russel R. Windes, the
editor of this series, who made his editorial suggestions as though
the writer were a mature human being. My wife's patience through
the writing of the manuscript and the co-operation of my children in
running to the local stationer for paper, typewriter ribbons, etc., also
deserve a warm "thank you."

Editor's foreword

As Professor Phillips points out in this volume, the small group has become the most common setting for speech communication. Most instructors of speech have consequently recognized the necessity of introducing the student to the theories and methods of group communication. In most departments the basic course in speech includes "discussion." Additionally, speech curricula include courses in discussion, group communication, and group leadership and dynamics.

Teaching group communication as a unit in the basic speech course is a difficult task. While instructors feel that a knowledge of theories and concepts of group behavior is essential, they are confronted with student demands for techniques of procedure. There is usually little time to lecture in depth. Textbooks are not always helpful, because their chapters on group communication are often too brief to discuss adequately both theory and implementation. The many excellent books devoted exclusively to group discussion are far too lengthy and complex to require of a beginning student. Monographs in sociology and social psychology are often too esoteric for a college freshman.

Professor Phillips' book is an attempt to bridge the gap between what experts know about small groups and what may be taught in a beginning course. He strikes a balance between theory and technique. His practical suggestions lean heavily on the insights and findings of the researchers. None of this is to suggest that this book is an unhappy but necessary compromise. To the contrary, it makes important contributions to the literature of small group communication. Of particular note is his attempt to establish standards by which the effectiveness of problem-solving groups may be judged. He outlines a system whereby groups can evaluate the potential effectiveness of their solutions. He discusses the various tools and methodologies for the analysis of small-group behavior, and relates these theories to classroom discussion. He considers the non-problem-solving group as well as the group that must address itself to a specific problem. He popularizes for the first time the concept of **game theory** in examining group interactions.

Professor Phillips' book should enable the student to do a competent and sensitive job in group communication. It enhances the student's skills through making him knowledgeable in the theories of group dynamics.

Russel R. Windes

Contents

List of figures

Communication and the small group

ONE

The small group in our society

Sociologist and social psychologist alike study how men interact with one another. The key to understanding our society and its problems is the unit of human interaction known as the "small group."

There is no specific number of people that makes a group "small." Generally, a small group is two or more people communicating with each other, face to face. They are better identified by their function than by their size.

Small groups operate all around us. In industry, for example, boards of directors plan over-all policy for a company. They attempt to solve major problems and pass down general statements of policy for management to interpret and carry out. The administrative levels are responsible for implementation of policy. They must usually find their own methods of dealing with problems of competition, production, distribution, sales, advertising, public relations, and personnel as they occur, subject to the guidelines passed down from the board. Management, in turn, diffuses some authority to lower administrative levels, like the various company departments. Each subdivision is responsible for carrying out policy in its own sphere. Management may be a little more rigid in its expectations of compliance with policy than the board of directors, but each administrative unit must solve its own problems as they occur. The work of the subdivisions must be co-ordinated, and this, too, requires a planning group. On each level, small groups of people work together to solve problems.

There is virtually no way an employee can avoid participation in group activity. Even the blue-collar worker gets involved as both labor and management seek ideas and information from him.

Federal, state, and local government operate in essentially similar fashion. Policy is made by a legislative body for administrators to carry out. Legislative, executive, and judicial branches of government each utilize small groups. The legislature, for example, employs investigating committees. Though these committees received a black eye during the 1950's for alleged malpractices, they are vital to the lawmaking process. It is necessary for legislators to have complete and pertinent information about problems before attempting to write laws. It would be impossible for them to do their job without small groups of fact gatherers assisting them. Groups of experts are often used to examine precedent and opinion to help judges to make their decisions. Administrative branches employ small groups very much like industry.

In education, small-group discussion is widely used in the classroom. School children first encounter the small group in elementary school when they participate in "sharing." More sophisticated assignments are introduced on every level, up to and including graduate school. The seminar is a good example of a small group engaged in learning. Most students make early contact with the committee system through their extracurricular activities. They learn about face-to-face interaction as they meet their counselor or adviser.

Outside of formal education, study and action groups like the Great Books or the League of Women Voters utilize discussion methods. The League of Women Voters is an excellent example. Small, local units examine current issues and recommend items for national study. Community-wide groups of the League explore the recommendations and select the topics they feel should be discussed by everyone. Once national topics have been selected, local units commence independent study. In Great Books, group members have a chance to share insights and ideas with others, to question and criticize in order to broaden their understanding of literature.

There is probably no more dramatic use of the small group than in therapy. Social workers rehabilitate groups of economically and culturally deprived people. Psychiatrists and psychologists employ group techniques to assist disturbed persons in anchoring themselves to others in their society. Groups are formed of parents of children with esoteric diseases to exchange information and provide social support. Speech clinicians use the small group to retrain stutterers and other speech defectives. The small group is a powerful tool in the treatment of many disabilities.

Most people participate in small-group activity formally and informally. If their jobs or their academic interests do not require small-group interaction, their social life certainly does, for people simply conversing about the weather or the prospects of their favorite ball team also employ the methods of the small group. Our society may reasonably be described as a large group made up of small groups. No educated person in a responsible position can avoid participation; for this reason, understanding of the small group is essential.

The nature of the small group

In order to understand how decisions are made and how people interact, it is necessary to examine the nature and function of the small group. In our society, we are confronted with a bewildering complexity of interacting organizations. Private social conversations can influence legislation. Legislation can direct business activity. Whenever a group of people comes together, for whatever reason, there is a potential for action. Decisions can be made; friendships or hostilities can develop. An understanding of how groups operate enhances the potential for influence. Many people are not able to participate in decision making in our society because they do not understand their appropriate role in a small group.

Suppose that a city council received a proposal to require installation of air-pollution-abatement devices on the machinery of all factories. The final step in the decision process would be a vote of the members to accept or reject the bill. The idea, however, may have originated from many sources:

1. A group of scientists at the local university determined through experiments that the atmosphere was "polluted."
2. A woman's civic group studied the problem of air pollution and decided something should be done locally.

3. A business group discovered that new industry was not locating in the area because of the pollution problem.
4. A group of influential men at the country club expressed concern about possible loss of outdoor recreation because of pollution.

Eventually members of these groups came together and organized a lobbying group to work for the passage of the bill. To do this, they framed a proposal which satisfactorily synthesized the divergent goals of the members. They worked together as problem solvers by studying other communities with similar problems as well as the problems in their local community. They concerned themselves with who would be affected by legislation and in what way. They surveyed the amount of money and personnel available for enforcement and the possible impact on the future of the community. Opposing views were reconciled and conflicts resolved. After a long time, a subcommittee drafted a proposal which was submitted to an attorney for examination so that it would be legally sound. Finally, a sympathetic councilman was found to propose the bill in council.

As soon as the bill was formally proposed, it was referred for study. The committee members were concerned with possible ramifications of the proposal. To broaden their knowledge, they held hearings, to which they invited representatives of the proposing group, as well as opponents, and anyone else who felt able to offer some pertinent information about the bill. In the light of their discoveries, they revised and re-introduced the proposal. After debate, in which each council member had an opportunity to express himself, the bill was voted on. Up to the final disposition of the bill, work was done by small groups.

On every level, as people came together to discuss air pollution, there was a purpose for the gathering and some outcome anticipated. Groups came together to socialize and enjoy the goodwill that comes from interaction. But more than this, they had a goal, both individual members and groups. Each was confronted with the problems of obtaining information, reconciling differences, and finding areas of agreement that would represent the feeling of the group. Since only the legislators had the power to enact law, only they had to be concerned with the protocol of voting. The other groups had a different problem—they had to be concerned with building as solid a consensus as possible.

Consensus as a group goal

Early in 1961, a national patriotic organization passed a resolution at their convention which read:

> Whereas a curious formula for arriving at decisions in the name of the group is currently being advanced and taught within the United States in various conferences, workshops, and agencies, relying upon a concept of group consensus which excuses the individual from defined responsibility and ignores established individual rights and which appears to signify a general weakening of the sense of personal responsibility within the nation: Resolved that the _____ dedicate its firm opposition to any method or concept of decision-making which encourages or implies the evasion, disregard, or reflection of the individual's personal responsibility. Resolved: that the _____ alert its members and the public to the importance of adhering to the time-tested principles of Parliamentary Procedure which are the instruments protecting the rights of the majority, the minority, and the individual that are essential to a free people.

The resolution was directed against "group dynamics" or any other method of decision making which employed consensus.

The defense of parliamentary procedure as a means of decision making is pertinent in the context of the development of American democracy. The one-man, one-vote, majority-rule precept has been the foundation of our democratic process. However, this system is applicable only to final decisions. Before a decision can be made on a course of action, a proposal must be derived from somewhere. Development of the proposal exemplifies a different phase of the decision-making process. The attack on "consensus" was unjustified because the patriotic organization did not understand the relationship between derivation of decisions and decision making.

The word "consensus" refers to the distinguishing feature of the small group, any group of two or more people who, for a given period of time, are concerned with a mutual goal and who devote their efforts during this time to the achievement of that goal. A social group may have as their goal simply staying together without friction. A legislative group may have to decide on a course of action. A problem-solving group seeks agreement about a solution to a problem or an evaluation of an idea. Such agreement without the formality of voting is referred to as "consensus."

Sometimes consensus is built on agreements about minor points over a period of time. Sometimes it is a major insight that suddenly reveals a solution that all members can accept. Consensus is the result of careful interpersonal communication in which members subordinate some of their personal feelings and desires to demonstrated facts or necessity. This is the reason, perhaps, that the patriotic organization felt so strongly about consensus. The basic idea is that some personal preferences must be surrendered to the welfare of the group. The minority must not sulk in silent opposition. It must be reconciled. The final agreement must include the ideas of all. If a member cannot accept the consensus, he may have to leave the group. Even if he did not agree totally, he would have to accept the fact that the consensus defines the group's "culture." A group defined in this context, is "those people who adhere to a similar set of ideas or principles, or who advocate the achievement of certain goals, though possibly disagreeing about means of implementation of their desires." Often, there is considerable harmony when a group comes together for the first time. Sometimes consensus does not result until after much interaction. Normally, members are able to reconcile the views of dissenting members. If they cannot, new groupings are made, and attempts to achieve consensus are renewed.

The unique role of small groups in a democratic society

Aristotle opens his classic work, **The Rhetoric,** with the statement, "Rhetoric is the counterpart of dialectic."[1] He then defines further: "Rhetoric is the art of finding in any given case all the available means of persuasion." The underlying assumption of Aristotle's philosophy was that man, as a rational being, could discover "truth," provided he had an opportunity to hear all sides of propositions expressed in equivalent fashion in a rhetorical mode.

Dialectic, or ". . . the art or practice of logical discussion as employed in investigating truth,"[2] was another method of discovery based on the Platonic ideal that no man ought to speak unless he understood the truth of his proposition.

---

[1]Aristotle, **The Rhetoric,** ed. Lane Cooper (New York: Appleton-Century-Crofts, 1932), p. 1.
[2]Clarence Barnhart, ed., **American College Encyclopedic Dictionary** (Chicago: The Spencer Press, 1959), p. 334.

Without trying to resolve the philosophical problem of the meaning of "truth," the dialectical mode can be described as a method of seeking a proposition to solve a problem, in contrast to the rhetorical mode, which is a method of seeking acceptance for a proposition. The two operations are complementary, particularly in the democratic tradition. One method seeks to discover an optimum solution; the other seeks to obtain assent from legitimate authorities to make it operational. The processes overlap. The rhetorician must observe many of the strictures of the dialectical mode as he investigates propositions. The dialectical process cannot be entirely free from persuasion, particularly in evaluative stages, when individual preferences of group members must be heard and synthesized.

Rhetoric and dialectic may be found in all types of societies. In authoritarian societies, however, they take a different form and serve a different purpose. In a democratic state, small groups make decisions and plan for implementation. In authoritarian societies, small groups serve in an advisory capacity and supervise implementation.

The extent to which individuals can influence decision making is the real distinction between a democratic and authoritarian state. The liberalization of government in the Western democracies stimulated a desire in the people to play a more significant role in decision making. The series of conferences and meetings held by President Johnson prior to his decision to increase the American commitment in Viet Nam in July, 1965 illustrates how the small group can influence decision making. Such use of advisory groups is common, as evidenced by the various "White House Conferences" on everything from drug addiction to higher education.

In authoritarian societies, a small group may act as ruler, as in the case of the military junta that ran the Dominican Republic after the overthrow of Juan Bosch in the summer of 1965. In such cases, there is no way of knowing how the group arrives at its decisions, for a "united front" is presented at all times, and dissenting members drop quietly from view.

Many critics of our society comment that we are hyperorganized today. Some deplore the state of affairs and complain that we are losing our individuality. Others contend that there is no better way to preserve individuality than to have an opportunity to influence the decisions that affect us. There is no question, however, about the fact that our American society is thoroughly organized and small group methods dominate our decision-making, problem-solving, and information-seeking activities.

The influence of John Dewey

The philosophical framework of the discussion process as it is currently used came from the work of John Dewey, particularly in the book, **How We Think.**[3] In this book, Dewey attempts to describe, not prescribe, the thought processes of a human being confronted with a problem. Dewey was concerned with "reflective" or "rational" thinking, goal-directed thinking, or problem solving. The pattern he described can be applied to any process of rational thought. Even creative insight will conform to part of the Dewey model.

According to Dewey, thinking begins with a feeling of perplexity, doubt, or confusion. Psychiatrists would refer to this as a "tension state," in which some drive or desire is frustrated. The individual attempts to eliminate the difficulty. To do this, it is necessary to follow a rational procedure, for acceptance of the first obvious solution could be "uncritical" and result in searching for solutions to the "wrong" problem.

Reflective thinking requires maintenance of a state of doubt while carrying on a systematic inquiry. Reflective thinking is characterized by deliberation and avoidance of impulsive acts. A reflective thinker consciously eliminates impediments to rational thought. He does not depend on a single authority to the exclusion of other possible sources of information. He attempts to keep his mind open to the greatest possible number of ideas. He seeks experience with many ways of doing things in order to broaden his range of choices. He resists spontaneous decisions. Reflective thinking is an active process requiring effort, consisting, according to Dewey, of "five phases":

1. The recognition of a difficulty.
2. Definition or specification of the difficulty.
3. Raising suggestions for possible solutions and rational exploration of the ideas.
4. Selection of an optimum solution from among many proposals.
5. Carrying out the solution.

For example, a student announces to his adviser that he is drop-

[3]John Dewey, **How We Think** (Boston: D. C. Heath, 1933).

ping out of school. The adviser recognizes this as a "feeling of difficulty." The problem is specified as "lack of funds." The student recognizes his decision to leave school was premature and only one of many possibilities. Other suggestions might be that he get a job, win a scholarship, negotiate a loan, write home for more money. The optimum solution is described as one that will keep the student in school without unnecessarily jeopardizing his grades. Getting money from home is rejected because the family exchequer is depleted. A scholarship is impossible because grades are not high enough. A job would take up too much study time. Loan funds are available, however, and this is selected as the course of action. The discovery of the rational solution proceeded through the five steps and produced a more satisfactory decision than the impulsive decision to drop out of school.

Dewey's "five phases of reflective thought" exerted a major influence on those men who were attempting to develop a rationale and method for training students in small-group processes. Sociologists concentrated their efforts on understanding the interpersonal dynamics of existing groups. Specialists in speech attempted to develop a method of training people in effective participation in small groups.

The work of early contributors in the field of speech led to the development of what might be called a "standard agenda" for discussion. Based on Dewey's model, the agenda consisted of steps that a group must take in order to arrive at a rational decision. These steps begin with Dewey's step 2—definition of a difficulty— and divide the subsequent steps into parts, ending just short of putting the solution into operation. The agenda looks like this:

I. **Definition of the Problem**
   A. Definition of the Terms of the Problem
   B. Definition of the Scope and Limits of the Problem
II. **Analysis of the Problem**
   A. Examination of the Factual Nature of the Problem
   B. Development of Causal Relations
   C. Criteria for Evaluation of Solutions
III. **Proposing Possible Solutions**
IV. **Testing Solutions Against Criteria**
V. **Selection or Construction of a Single Final Solution**

Sometimes a sixth step is added:

VI. **Suggestions for Putting Solutions into Operation**

Formal group discussion begins with a problem question. The question is generally phrased in open-ended fashion. Propositions which allow choice between only two alternatives are not suitable for discussion. A group can legitimately discuss questions like, "What can be done to improve school spirit?" A question phrased, "Should we abolish student government?" allows the group to select only one of two mutually exclusive choices. The purpose of open-ended wording is to prevent question-begging solutions.

A careful analysis of the question comes next. If the group is to discuss "the influence of Faulkner on American literature," some restriction must be placed on the discussion. The words "influence" and "American literature" must be defined or explained. Gathering pertinent information about the question helps explicate the question for the group.

Evaluation of causes is imperative. The group working on the problem of "school spirit" must be able to describe events and conditions that led to the conclusion that school spirit was deficient. They must also be able to state concrete reasons why the conditions occurred. The group attempting to assess Faulkner must explore reasons why experts and laymen are interested in his writing.

Precise statements must be made, against which solutions can be evaluated. Such statements help the members measure their progress and serve to indicate when they are done. As each solution is proposed, it can be tested against criterion statements. The solution that meets the criteria best is selected as a final report. Thus, the major steps in Dewey's thought-process model are built into a logical agenda that a group can use for exploring all types of problems. No group need adhere rigidly to an agenda. Dewey did not prescribe a method of thought. Rather, he attempted to describe how rational thought took place. When his system is applied to discussion, it merely means that somewhere in the discussion, each of the steps, not necessarily in order, must take place. In some cases steps are emphasized; in other cases they are given minimal treatment.

The final step of the Dewey format was added by the field of industrial management. Executives are fundamentally concerned with final results. It was necessary for them to devise a method to use in developing plans of operation that could be used by small groups. The most current of such techniques is called PERT, an acronym for Program Evaluation and Review Technique. This system was developed as a response to problems in managing the construction of the Polaris guided missile, and is currently being used by most government agencies. It is required of all companies contracting with the United States Government.

PERT is a probabilities-based system which involves administrative and operations personnel on all levels in the development of program plans. We will deal with it in detail in Chapter Four. PERT is applied to the group process in problem solving immediately after a solution has been accepted by the group. If the solution is in the form of a program, PERT is used to devise the plan of procedure. One of the major advantages of using PERT is that it requires the problem-solving group to think in practical terms as they work toward solutions. Recent experimentation with PERT as a final step of the discussion process seems to demonstrate that it is the logical completion of the Dewey system applied to group problem solving.[4]

The "five phases of reflective thought" apply to all forms of group interaction. Each time a group comes together, they must have a purpose. Their success is measured by the extent to which they achieve their purpose. A social group, for example, may have as its purpose avoiding conflict for a period of time. An educational group may seek greater understanding of a concept or idea. A problem-solving group may be required to produce a fully detailed program. In any case, awareness of the requirements of reflective thought enables the group to apply them to its unique problem in such a way that the most useful solution results.

Sources of small groups

In authoritarian societies, small groups serve in advisory capacities or are charged with developing implementation plans. Final decisions are reserved for the governing authority. In rare cases, a group may serve as ruler but generally the scope of power of small groups is restricted.

In a democracy, small groups engage in activities ranging from casual socialization to major decision making. To a very great extent, major government policy is determined by small groups. The advisers that counseled and encouraged President John Kennedy before the "Bay of Pigs" fiasco were a small group. So were the men who urged him to select Lyndon Johnson as his running mate.

Extension of patterns of small-group problem solving may be con-

[4]Gerald M. Phillips, "PERT as a Logical Adjunct to the Discussion Process," *Journal of Communication*, XV (June 1965), 89–99.

sidered one of the positive signs of a mature, democratic society. The small group offers the individual member the opportunity to influence decision making to the full extent of his capabilities and interests. He can free himself from authoritarian control and become more than a mere anonymous member of the electorate. Small-group activity increases his choices, whereas the parliamentary system offers him only two choices. A compromise requiring concessions by a minority to a majority is not necessary, because small groups are composed of more than majorities and minorities wrangling over a single proposition. The group may "tailor-make" a solution to fit both their problem **and** the pleasure of the members. There is no need for factionalism, for a spirit of co-operative inquiry pervades the process.

Of course, the foregoing is an idealistic view of the small group. Few, if any, groups live up to the hopes and dreams of optimistic small-group theorists. Furthermore, our society is still imperfect. Many citizens are denied the privilege of influencing decision making because of their economic status or color. However, the small group has sufficiently proved itself as a therapeutic, evaluative, and problem-solving method so that it must be understood by anyone who hopes to be a productive member of an impressively complex technological democracy.

There are six principle ways in which small groups come together. Each of these is a function of the motivations of the group members.

The casual group. At any social gathering, knots of people will be found conversing about matters of mutual interest. Groups of this sort do not seek agreement on statements of policy. Rather, their purpose is to exchange ideas and extend the warmth of companionship. Conversation can ramble over many topics. It is not necessary that the group stay on the track. Participants may enter and leave as they choose. Some people will move from group to group. Others will station themselves and become focal points of conversation. In order to hold conversational groups together, some topics are declared "taboo." These are usually topics that may stimulate hostility or conflict. If a member raises a forbidden topic, there is a scurry to change the subject. The members of the group have a tacit consensus that staying together in friendly companionship is their goal and will resist any threat to that status.

The self-motivated group. The self-motivated group is composed of people who have independently recognized that a problem exists and decided that action should be taken. They may be concerned about the sale of pornographic literature on local newsstands, or they may wish to protest an action of the government. The group is pulled together, initially, by a prime mover who feels strongly about the issue. Some people invited to the first meeting will discover that they do not agree with the rest of the group and will either go away and remain silent, or try to form a group to represent their own views. Others will find that though they agree with the group's aims and objectives, they do not agree strongly enough to justify further involvement. Eventually a structure will emerge: a homogeneous aggregate of people who agree about goals, though not necessarily about the means of achieving them. Their problem will be to discover the ways to accomplish their objectives. They may discover that it is necessary to become a "public relations" or "lobbying" group even after they have agreed on a proposal. In order to perpetuate their program, once achieved, it might be necessary for them to establish a permanent organization. Regular employees will then be charged with carrying on the program whereas the original group establishes lines of policy. The self-motivated group will have changed to an ongoing group.

The ongoing group. Personnel of an ongoing group hold their membership by virtue of an occupational title. They are the managers, researchers, clerks, and executives of permanent organizations. Within each organizational structure, small groups are charged with responsibility for developing and carrying out operations. In a manufacturing concern, for example, small groups will be concerned with obtaining raw materials, manufacturing, sales, and financial matters. At the top there will be a coordinating body which lays down the rules under which the subordinates must operate. If the organization has stockholders, selection of the directors is done by vote. Throughout the organization, groups both establish policy and prepare and supervise plans to execute it. Groups are permanently organized and solve problems as they arise as a regular routine.

The appointment group. Some groups come together because they have been selected for their special skills or interests to solve designated problems. The regular and special committees of organizations are examples of this type of group. Members are appointed by an executive body and serve for a limited time. Even if the committee is permanent, the membership need not be.

The committee system can be found in virtually every aspect of society. Fact-finding committees prepare special reports for lawmakers or business executives. Program committees plan a schedule of activities for the Rotary Club or the P.T.A. Committees evaluate the severity of problems and recommend those that seem to demand immediate attention. Groups of this type represent the most pervasive application of the small group in our society. They can be regarded as thoroughly democratic attempts to diffuse the responsibility for decision making.

The educational group. Some study groups arise spontaneously. A group of neighbors may decide to organize a book-review club or to meet regularly to consider community problems. Most, however, are ongoing. In the League of Women Voters, for example, the local unit is permanent and varies only in the problems it considers. Great Books retains a standard structure, changing only the books under discussion. In each case, membership is voluntary.

In classrooms, teachers may elect to use a small-group format to enhance understanding of complex ideas and concepts. Though participation is mandatory, the group approach to learning can materially alter the atmosphere of the classroom and improve rapport between teacher and student.

The therapeutic group. The small group is used extensively in therapy. Psychiatrists, psychologists, speech therapists, and social workers employ group techniques in their treatment of personal and social disorders. This type of group cannot be studied in precisely the same dimensions as problem-solving or educational groups. Concentration is on the personal improvement, change in behavior, or alteration of values of the individual members. There is no collective group goal. Members of therapy groups seek solutions to their own problems. The group is used as an aid to discovery. Interactions between the members facilitate mutual support.

The interpersonal transaction in a problem-solving or educational group can, in the same fashion, have a healthy effect on the personalities of group members. There is, apparently, something about the atmosphere of the small group that makes it conducive both to individual and group problem solving. For this reason, many authorities on small groups are concerned with the effect of the group on the individual, as well as the individual's effect on the output of the group. Much small-group literature is devoted to study of alterations in personality and behavior of persons that take place in a group context. This emphasis in research has taken precedence over the study of the output of groups as they seek to solve problems. This book is concerned with both interpersonal relations in groups and group output. It should be clearly understood that the personality of the members of the group has a great deal to do with the effectiveness of the group, and the atmosphere of group problem solving has an effect, often a therapeutic one, on the personalities of the individual members. Furthermore, most groups must produce some sort of consensus. Sometimes excessive concentration on human relations impedes consensus, just as excessive concern with output results in a sacrifice of human values. Our interest is in both the group as a whole and the individuals of which it is composed.

Why study the small group?

The tool used by groups is language. By interchange of ideas and information, individuals can pool their resources and work toward accomplishment of collective goals. The communication situation encountered by members of small groups is different from that of a public speaker. The public speaker seeks to convey information, inculcate belief, incite to action, or induce emotion. Ideally, members of small groups work toward cooperative participation in an effort to achieve consensus. The ideal situation, however, often does not exist in reality. Many members of small groups use their colleagues as audiences whom they attempt to motivate into thinking precisely as they do.

It would be unreasonable to believe that merely telling people to modify their attitudes when they participate in small groups would be sufficient to bring about desired behavior change. The atmosphere of the small group, nevertheless, does seem to bring about a natural change in the communication patterns of members. Those who have a group orientation are not favorably disposed toward receipt of persuasive messages, and any overt attempts by individuals to dominate the group usually meet with rejection. Such domination that does come about is usually the result of lack of interest on the part of group members, which allows an advocate to dominate.

There is also the possibility of overco-operation, a situation where each member of the group is so solicitous of the feelings of others that no direct action can be taken for fear of offending someone.

It is necessary to examine the communication process in the small group to determine what behavior leads to successful and unsuccessful outcomes. The process of problem solving must be studied in order to discover how groups may be assisted in solving problems and how individual group members can be better trained. Most important, understanding the small group helps us understand the structure of our society.

Some groups make provision for systematic self-study by appointing a member to keep track of constructive and destructive intragroup events. He is called upon to offer periodic critiques in the hope that this feedback will help the group avoid pitfalls in their subsequent discussion. This procedure is customarily used in classes in group discussion where the teacher serves as observer-critic.

Much the same procedure is used in therapy groups, but the observer is a trained clinician who assists the group members as individuals to see themselves more clearly in the light of their interactions with others.

Systematic study of the discussion process will lead to the development of refined methods for training group members. There is no formula yet devised that will guarantee success in small groups by individual members or success of a whole group in achieving its goal. Much more information is needed, particularly by those who participate, for one thing is certain: those who understand something about the group and its problems and are able to translate their knowledge into action are highly desirable group members, capable of disseminating their learning merely by their relationships with other members.

The small group has been extensively studied, and there are many thorough compilations of research findings. Several of these are listed in the bibliography. The emphasis of research to date has been on internal processes of the group, on the assumption that awareness of what goes on inside the group will lead to interpersonal involvement and subsequent improvement of outcome. In the following chapters we will attempt to summarize something of what is known about small groups and the ways people participate in them, as well as to offer formats for educational, therapeutic, and problem-solving group discussion.

TWO

Understanding the small group

A small group is an entity with a style and personality. It is made up of individual human beings, each of whom brings to it his own personality, values, feelings, and life history. When the individuals combine, the group becomes something more than the sum total of individual behaviors. Each member influences the group, and is in turn influenced by it. Several factors, including problem types, individual personality, leadership, communication patterns, and group size, exert an influence on the activity of the group as a whole. In this chapter we will examine these influences as well as the types of research that have enabled us to learn what we know about small groups. In Chapter Five we will discuss the ways in which people interact in the group.

Influence of problem type on the effectiveness of the group

The type of problem a group deals with partially determines its goals, style of operation, and form of solution. The dimensions in which a group can work are laid out by the type of problem. Attention of members is initially focused on goals in terms of the problem they encounter.

Fact-finding groups must be task-oriented and highly critical. The purpose of a fact-finding group is to discover as much information about the problem as possible. Their task includes gathering relevant opinions from competent authorities, as well. They do not evaluate either the facts or the opinions; they merely gather and organize the data.

Fact finding must be approached with a desire to discover "truth" insofar as it can be found. The group must also recognize that their job has limits, for it is impossible to gather **all** the facts about anything.

Fact finding is the basis for the subsequent steps in discussion. Most groups begin examination of their problem by surveying factual information. Groups that desire to evaluate a situation need information on which to base their judgments. Policy makers require a solid basis of knowledge about their problem. Educational groups need basic data as a framework for conceptual learning. A clinician involved in group therapy requires basic information about symptoms and behavior of the members of his group.

Some examples of fact-finding groups are legislative researchers, the people who prepare annual reports of businesses, committees to prepare information reports for civic groups, etc. Most policy-making groups must go through a fact-finding phase unless some other group has done the job for them.

A fact-finding group is a task group. Its only concern with policy is the answer to the procedural question, "How can we best gather a sufficient quantity of relevant information?" It is difficult for one person to gather adequate information on a complex problem. Several people, however, may pool fact-finding tasks in such a way that the important sources of information are thoroughly explored. Jobs can be distributed commensurate with the qualifications and interests of the members. The group decides on the manner of task assignment.

Once facts have been gathered, the whole group tests them for adequacy, bias, completeness, relevance, and currency. Those facts that "measure up" must be organized so that they are of maximum use to the group that will eventually use them in evaluation or policy making.

Fact-finding groups are characterized by efficiency. Members attempt to avoid reacting to facts. Conflict, if it occurs at all, should be over whether or not a statement is a fact. The chief obstacle to successful fact finding is impatience. Since facts must be painstakingly analyzed, to avoid boredom members may find themselves evaluating or precipitating a discussion of conclusions irrelevant to the task at hand. This tends to distort the facts, and members may find themselves engaging in various forms of advocacy. It is imperative that fact-finding groups remember that others are dependent on their information. They must be as objective as possible.

Evaluation groups must understand the purpose of their task. Special groups are often established to review problems to determine their severity. They must decide whether a problem demands immediate attention, or if parts or all of the problem can be ignored. Such groups may also be requested to discover causes of a problem and to assist the activities of a policy-making body. If an organization is faced with several problems, an evaluation group may determine the order in which they are dealt with. An example of an evaluation group would be the "Ten-year Committee" of a university making recommendations about the relative importance of a wide variety of problems to administrative decision makers.

Most educational groups are evaluative in their activities. Their assessment of the quality of types of literature or severity of political problems cannot extend to policy making for they do not have the authority or involvement to warrant the development of solutions. Sometimes educational problems do not demand solutions, but are phrased to provide group members with an opportunity to utilize their knowledge in gaining an understanding of a situation or idea.

An evaluation group cannot go beyond the limits of the facts at its disposal. If the fact-finding group that has preceded it has prepared a useful report, the evaluation group has the best chance to be judicious in analyzing the information. When evaluation groups are required to make decisions based on scanty or biased information, their recommendations are not useful.

Policy-making groups are concerned with "output" in the form of a program. Customarily, fact finding and evaluation are the responsibility of the policy-making group. A learning group may not need to go beyond the evaluation phase. A history class discussing the causes of the Korean War need not present proposals to "solve a problem." Rather, their examination of the facts should lead them to a judgment about the wisdom and efficacy of the action taken.

Policy-making is the task most often allotted to small groups. Fact finding and evaluation precede the development of policy. Policy making begins with a general statement of a problem and progresses through rational steps to a solution. The solution may be a general declaration of policy or a detailed program.

The "standard agenda" is the format customarily employed. While the steps of the standard agenda need not be followed in exact order, policy-making groups often find is necessary to pass through all of them. Variations can be introduced where necessary. The group must be concerned with the discovery of a suitable solution and with the eventual application of the solution. Policy-making groups, as a rule, cover eight major points in their progress to a solution. The procedure will be considered in detail in Chapter Four.

Specification. The group defines the terms of the question and agrees on the limits of the problem.

Fact finding. The group marshals facts relevant to the problem, analyzes the situation, and redefines the problem in the light of the facts.

Determination of causes. The group discovers the reasons why conditions are as they are, and decides whether the problem calls for symptomatic or causal treatment.

Approval of criteria and goals. The group ascertains the scope of its authority, clarifies who will administer the program, evaluates resources, stipulates its moral, legal, and practical limitations, and agrees on a statement about what is to be accomplished. These statements serve as references against which proposals can be tested.

Proposal of solutions. Several solutions are proposed and tested against the goals. A final solution is derived either by selecting one of the proposed solutions or by synthesizing a solution out of bits and pieces of various proposals.

Operation planning. Some groups are responsible for preparing a plan by which solutions can be put into effect. If the group does not have this responsibility, they must still consider the practical consequences of their solution and be prepared to present proposals for overcoming obstacles to implementation.

Actuation. The solution and operation plans, where required, are turned over to an administrative authority, which does what is recommended.

Evaluation. At some later date, the group checks its work to determine how well their program has met the objectives set for it.

Though rigid adherence to the agenda is not necessary, it affords a useful check list of what the group must do. Naturally, each policy-making group must make its own adjustments. Agenda need not be explicit as long as the group follows a logical plan.

Program-implementation groups utilize modern cybernetic technology. The use of groups to plan program implementation is a new development in problem solving. (The first recorded use of such a group was in 1958 during the construction of the Polaris guided missile.) An implementation group pools information to plan operations as efficiently as possible. In industry and government, operation groups work closely with computer teams who use cybernetic techniques to obtain estimates of the likelihood of success for a program. Given proper data, the computer can isolate critical points in the program, offer a critique of the deployment of materiel and personnel, and provide guidelines on which an administrator can base decisions. PERT and CPM are the two most widely used systems. They are currently being applied to problem solving in small groups and have been found useful in agencies with limited manpower and resources. PERT planning will be discussed in Chapter Four.

Educational groups must amplify understanding of ideas. The purpose of discussion in education is to enhance conceptual understanding by individual group members. Such groups are not helpful in mastering factual information. Rather, they provide a method for students to integrate facts and test their ability to apply them. Educational groups make extensive use of specialized techniques. Some of these methods will be discussed in Chapter Three.

Adherence to formal procedures is not of great importance in educational discussion. The guiding principle should be active participation in the learning process. Often, groups purporting to use discussion assign a member to give a "report" on a topic. The discussion itself is nothing more than a disorganized question period. This defeats the purpose of the discussion method as a pedagogical tool. If discussion is to be used in the classroom at all, it must have some purpose and be closely related to the material being studied, yet allow considerable leeway for expansion of the students' understanding.

Members of educational discussion groups should be encouraged rather than compelled to participate. Sufficient structure should be maintained so that no member feels inhibited because others dominate. All should be free to express their views. The instructor should not insist on ratification of his own ideas. Actually, no teacher should attempt the discussion method who is not prepared to entertain arguments against his own position, for the method, when well run, seems to encourage objections, controversy, dissension, and the expression of "wild" ideas. If the teacher takes an active part, he may intimidate the students. If he participates on their level, he may lose his classroom authority. He must be prepared to play the role of recorder-observer with minimal intervention.

Academic courses in discussion and small groups are generally taught by the discussion method. Students may be given the responsibility of preparing and implementing their own syllabus. Grading may even be left to the discretion of the group, subject only to basic restrictions imposed by the school. When this sort of thing is first attempted, the instructor must be prepared for long, embarrassed periods of silence, followed by disbelief and objection by the students. Most of them are not really prepared to accept the responsibility of free decision making. Placing them in the position where they must do it is the best method of teaching them how it is done.

It is virtually impossible to evaluate participation in educational discussion, for what the student acquires is internal. It is irrelevant to evaluate the output of the discussion, for it is incidental to what the student has learned. Objective tests of material covered in discussion cannot tell the story accurately, although there is evidence that courses taught by the discussion method result in at least as much subject matter mastery as those taught by the traditional lecture-recitation. The real gain, however, is inside the student. It can only be measured by the participant in terms of the expansion of his understanding and appreciation of the subject.

Therapy groups have personality change as their goal. The use of the small group for therapy purposes was stimulated by the fact that people with problems feel somewhat better when they understand that their misery is not exclusively their own. Group therapy is currently one of the most widely used methods of assisting people in overcoming or adjusting to their problems.

Nominally, the therapy group is controlled by a therapist. He cannot, however, exert the kind of control exercised by a problem-solving discussion leader. His responsibility is to guide, or more often, to accept and permit. At the start of group therapy, a permissive attitude by the therapist seems to encourage communication among the patients. When they discover that their remarks will not be challenged, they feel more comfortable about participating. On occasion, the therapist can prod silent members to help them get started. He must then quickly withdraw from the discussion and allow them to follow their own direction. He must, of course, act to protect any group member from excessive threat.

Sound diagnostic information can be obtained from the interactions in the therapeutic discussion. Diagnoses can then be fed back to the patients either in the group or privately. The most valuable therapy comes from the feeling the patients get that they are of use to others. The frankness and insight displayed by patients in therapy sessions is often far more valuable than many of the more formal private therapies.

Because the ends or outputs of therapeutic discussion are personal, there is almost no structure. Attempts to control or channel contributions may result in withdrawal from interaction. Permissiveness is most important. To a lay observer, group-therapy sessions often appear anarchic. The trained therapist, however, is aware of structure, even though he cannot impose it. The structure is not at all like that of problem solving, for it is imposed by the logic of the patient's interactions, and can be understood only by a participant.

One caution—beginners in group processes are often captivated by the techniques of group therapy. They are dangerous in the hands of untrained persons. The use of devices like psychodrama and nondirective therapy in the hands of a novice can do considerably more damage than good. Unless there is a very good reason to do otherwise, more traditional methods should be employed by the layman.

What the group desires to accomplish will partly determine its style. Whether the group uses a rigid agenda or functions loosely and permissively will be dictated by the needs of the group. If the group is required to produce a formal solution to a problem, it will require considerably more structure than if its goal is appreciation of literary material. Some attention to the necessary output will help the group decide on the amount of rigidity it can tolerate in its format.

The influence of personality types on discussion

The personality characteristics demanded of the good discussion participant are totally unattainable in any one person. Writers in the field list variously: knowledge of the topic, co-operativeness, optimism, critical ability, attention, empathy, moderation, sincerity, tentativeness, perseverance, sense of humor, goodwill, enthusiasm, etc., as traits "necessary" for successful participation. It is obvious that no one person can possess all of these or acquire them on demand. To understand the interpersonal dynamics of the discussion process, however, the influence of some major personality traits should be surveyed. In general, the output of a group can be improved if certain personality types are present. Negative personality types may offer severe impediments.

It is generally assumed that the group is something other than the "sum of its parts." That is, the group acquires unique characteristics which result from the interactions of the members. The aggregate of these traits can be called the "group personality." The group personality, once developed, will influence the way in which members participate. A group that has taken on a rigid, dogmatic personality will tend to suppress contributions and discourage creative members. An open, tolerant group will encourage communication, but may discourage efficient operation.

We will consider the influence of some of the major personality variables here. The problem of relationships between members will be considered in Chapter Five.

Intelligence. It is almost too obvious to assert that there must be intelligence present in the group in order to achieve an intelligent outcome. Members tend to respond to the group personality commensurate with their intelligence. If the atmosphere of the group seems, for example, to be restrictive, intelligent members are often discouraged, and reduce their contributions. The higher the intelligence, the better the individual will function in a permissive atmosphere. Not-so-intelligent members, however, seem to "muddle around" when placed in a permissive environment. Contribution by the more intelligent members tends to create a more intelligent group personality. Others members will be challenged to raise the level of their contributions.

A major problem faced by the intelligent member is his rising impatience with the protraction of the group process. It may seem to him that many of the group's problems could be solved (by him) very rapidly. But the group necessarily moves at the pace set by the greater number of participants, and often the intelligent person must wait until his ideas are understood by the rest of the members before he can move on to the next point.

Intelligence should not be confused with glibness. In a small group, the intelligent contributor is well prepared, alert to critical weaknesses, and able to identify obscure relationships. Intelligence cannot be measured by quantity of verbal output. Often, intelligent members capable of making worthwhile contributions remain silent while facile and shallow participants engage in superficial verbal byplay.

Intelligence in the group can be encouraged by urging advance preparation by members and by discouraging those who talk too much. Failure of intelligent, well-prepared members to participate may lead to perpetuation of ignorance. The group process, strong as it might be, cannot compensate for a dearth of discerning contributions. Intelligent people can be retained as motivated members by granting them a little leeway in their participation and allowing them to assume leadership roles where they desire.

Dogmatism—co-operativeness. Excessive dogmatism impedes the group process whereas the co-operative personality assists it. These axioms may seem simple enough, but they are not as clear-cut as they seem. On occasion, the group needs a touch of dogma to move it ahead. Sometimes the group may suffer from excessive co-operation, particularly when members strive to please each other rather than work toward the group goal.

In general, however, the person who is convinced that he is correct, and is unable to modify his ideas in any way impedes the group. His persuasive appeals disrupt the discussion, causing the group to split into two factions representing extreme, or "polar," attitudes. If the dogmatic person is in a position of authority, then the group falls entirely under his control and becomes a body of "yes-men" instead of a problem-solving group. Discussions led by such persons are nothing more than sycophancy sessions in which subordinates seek to discover what their dogmatic superior wants them to say and then feed it back to him. To interfere with the will of the dogmatic leader is to risk sanctions. The group process becomes an audience situation in which the members devote their time to feeding the ego of the authoritarian leader.

While it is undesirable for an individual to associate his personality with his ideas, it is not a good idea to attempt to avoid advocacy at all costs. If a discussion group is to make authentic progress, members must be encouraged to defend worthy ideas and propositions. Frank expression of belief by the members provides the substance of a strong consensus. Such advocacy should focus on the group goal or procedural needs of the group. Appeals to the welfare of individual members stimulate personality-based conflict. Advocates must show some willingness to modify their positions when it has been sufficiently demonstrated that they are no longer tenable. If one or more members plead their personal convictions against all comers, the discussion can become a debate about dogma. The group is thus prevented from examining a wide compass of ideas and consensus suffers from the limited exposure.

Willingness to co-operate has a healthy effect on the group outcome, but even it can be carried too far. The requirement that members must co-operate to achieve the group goal should not be construed to mean that every member must be thoroughly pleased with the outcome. The goal of group discussion is not merely avoidance of conflict. Though conflict is potentially destructive, it must not be avoided at all costs, for the strongest solutions are forged out of legitimate differences in opinion. Failure to disagree when disagreement is warranted may mean that the group is denied the chance to explore possible alternatives. Members who try excessively hard to please may make authoritarians out of those they are trying to please. Co-operativeness means exercise of the critical faculty in the interest of the group, as well as agreeing whenever possible. Members should avoid personal involvement with their own ideas, but there is no need to subordinate them to a notion of spurious harmony.

Empathy. One of the most valuable traits a member of a discussion group can have is the ability to empathize with the values of others. Empathy does not mean uncritical acceptance of the ideas of others, but rather an ability to "feel" why people believe as they do. The ability to understand why someone may hold strongly to a contrary opinion helps in determining what might be necessary to bring about a consensus.

It is easy to evaluate the behavior of others as "irrational." All behavior, however, must be regarded as rational in the eyes of the behaver at the time of behaving. There is a reason why people act and speak as they do, even though the reason might not be discernible to an observer.

Inability to empathize is a major source of conflict in small groups. Classification of the behavior of others as "irrational," "stupid," "destructive," "unco-operative," etc., leads to hostile responses which in turn evoke more hostility. An empathetic awareness tends to preclude evaluation. If evaluation of the behavior of others can be avoided, the chances for understanding are materially increased.

Regrettably, there is no way to learn empathy. Voluntary suppression of the results of lack of empathy is useful, however. If members can at least avoid verbalizing hostile judgments of others and perhaps suspend their tendency to evaluate invidiously, an aura of empathy can be created which may lead to genuine understanding between members.

Moderation–tentativeness. Ability to suspend judgment and avoid extreme positions are valuable attributes for small-group members. Advance commitment to a solution or adherence to a cause may stir up conflict that is difficult to resolve.

Problem-solving and educational groups seek consensus. Therapeutic groups require a calm atmosphere. In any event, if members can avoid jumping to conclusions and remain open-minded long enough to hear what is being said, the possibility of harmony within the group is increased.

Moderation on the part of group members is essential to success in problem solving. Moderation is indispensable to an attitude of tentativeness. If members enter a discussion with the solution firmly fixed in their minds, they may become intolerant of all other ideas. Moderate commitment permits members to discard their ideas without feeling that their personalities have been threatened when those ideas have been rejected by the group.

Criticality. A healthy critical attitude by each member assists the group in doing its job. Neither statements of fact nor opinion should be permitted to go unchallenged. Not all statements represented as factual are really facts, and not all opinions are acceptable, no matter how vehemently they are expressed. Some or all members must assume responsibility for questioning each contribution of fact or opinion and must continue to press the attack until the contributor has proved the worth of his offering.

A "show-and-tell" format is sometimes adopted by discussion groups. One member makes a statement. Everyone listens. Then the next person takes his turn, and so on until each member has spoken. Each contribution is unrelated to the one that preceded it. Co-operation means more than taking turns. Unwillingness of members to respond directly to the remarks of others may mean that they are still acting independently and have not yet associated themselves with the group goal. So long as no critical effort is exerted, each member can retain his beliefs intact. Intelligent criticism helps group members relate to each other, as well as to the group goal.

Unwillingness to be critical may stem from a misinterpretation of the requirements of consensus. A good discussion leader can set the proper tone by demonstrating how it is possible to question a statement of fact without calling the man who made it a "liar"; how an opinion can be challenged without calling the man who expressed it a "fool."

Criticality, like any virtue, can be carried to extremes. When critical comments are associated with personal attacks, conflict is stimulated. When critical remarks appear to be picayune, they may be directed to impeding the group's progress. Nevertheless, constructive criticism should be encouraged. It is easier to deal with a case of hypercriticality than it is to reach a satisfactory consensus in a discussion devoid of criticism.

Patience. Participation in discussion demands patience. Reaching a consensus sometimes seems to take inordinately long. It may appear that one person, working alone, could have solved the problem with a good deal less effort, and this is probably true. Organizations in which members have surrendered their decision-making power to a single authority can be highly efficient, if the members have chosen the right leader, and if he remains the person he was when he was chosen. Efficiency is purchased at the sacrifice of the independence of the members. Further, there is no check on the quality of solutions. Efficiency with a second-rate solution is not preferable to taking the time to discover the best possible solution. Moreover, higher-quality solutions may be administered more easily.

The group process, to be effective, must take into account the varying perspectives of the individual members of the group. Members act both as individuals and as representatives of attitudes they held outside the group. It is wise to take as much time as is necessary to give all members reasonable opportunity to present their points of view. The member who is not able to wait out the process often becomes an advocate, or tries to rush the group to a solution whatever way he can.

Patience comes with experience. Beginners at discussion can solve major world problems like peace and poverty in half an hour. Critical evaluation of their solutions, however, demonstrates that a little more time should have been allowed. Those people who cannot develop patience often run for office so they can appoint the committees rather than serve on them.

Communication skill. Certain basic skills are necessary to successful participation in a discussion group. Several of these will be discussed in detail in Chapter Three. Basically, a member's voice must be loud enough to be heard and his remarks organized well enough to be understood. Comments, in general, should be related to the topic of discussion. Beyond this, excessive concern for speech delivery may make a member too self-conscious to participate well.

Oral contributions cannot be evaluated quantitatively. It appears obvious that the person who says nothing contributes nothing to the discussion. This is not fully true, however, for nods and facial expressions can provide positive supports or negative cues to other participants. It is not always worthwhile to try to pry a contribution from a silent member. The old adage, "Still waters run deep," may not be appropriate. Some bodies of still water are stagnant. Silence in a member should not be interpreted positively or negatively. He may or may not have a contribution to make. If it is discovered that a member's silence is due to lack of interest or preparation it may be well to ignore him.

The person who talks a great deal may not really want to dominate the discussion. While it is often true that the man who talks a lot is seeking a leadership role, excessive verbal output may be motivated by sincere interest or a high level of preparation. Sometimes members find it necessary to step into a talk vacuum. If a few members of the group are participating, then, of course, their contribution will be proportionately greater. It is not unusual that persons who do the most talking get their own way. They may not be actively seeking control, but they achieve dominance because they are the only ones in the group willing to try. The group leader may often have to play "devil's advocate" to keep excessive talkers honest, particularly if no one else in the group is offering any challenge.

Leadership style as a determinant of group activity

There are four main leadership obligations that must be assumed either by a designated leader or by members of a discussion group.

Maintenance of adherence to some agenda. The leader must see to it that the group moves in relatively orderly fashion from starting point to conclusion. To do this, he must keep the group's activities centered around a series of more or less rational steps called the "agenda." The agenda need not be explicit. It may be an unspecified plan in the mind of the leader, or it may develop from the logic of the discussion topic. Its purpose is to guide the group to achievement of its goal, whatever it might be: a list of facts, a statement of evaluation, a policy, an understanding of ideas, an improvement in behavior. It is often useful to get the group to agree on an explicit agenda. This procedure seems to increase the attentiveness of the members. The agenda acts as a set of criteria by which the leader can assess the behavior of his group. Gross deviations from the agenda may block achievement of the group's objectives. If an agenda seems to be changing drastically, it may be necessary to take the time to reappraise the group's goals.

Traffic control. In all but a few unstructured types of discussion, the leader determines who speaks when. He creates the atmosphere for interpersonal communication. If he is excessively rigid and requires that members seek recognition before they speak, he risks an authoritarian atmosphere which might discourage participation by some members. If he is excessively loose and exerts no leadership at all, he may turn control of the group over to a few members, which might be equally discouraging.

Somehow, the individual who talks too much must be discouraged to the point where others can speak, without dampening his willingness to participate. The shy, diffident, reticent member must be given the impression that when he is ready to talk, his contributions will be welcome. The leader is initially responsible for the mood for verbal interchange, although his perspective must be supported by the members of his group. The leader cannot silence a garrulous member if it is the group's will that he continue speaking. No matter how much the leader may encourage wider participation, it will be ineffective unless members pick up his cue and begin to talk. Of course, if the group has developed its own atmosphere and seems satisfied with it, the leader will normally acquiesce and assist in the enforcement of the group's will.

The leader also breaks deadlocks—decides who talks, when more than one person tries at the same time. He must also fill in gaps of silence and attempt to prod the group into activity when the discussion seems to lag.

Resolution of conflict. No leader is capable of preventing all conflict, unless he is such an authoritarian that no freedom is possible. The leader, however, can specify ground rules so that conflict can be made constructive. He can discourage attacks on personalities and prevent polarization of the group into hostile factions. If a minority opinion is being thoroughly rejected, he can lend it support by temporary advocacy demonstrating that the view is worthy of expression and a hearing. If a majority is running roughshod over the remainder of the group, he can become the advocate for the minority and thus ensure adequate presentation of their views. He must understand that while his is the responsibility for control of conflict, he must rely on the members to support him. If he attempts to exert too much control, he may appear obnoxiously overdirective.

The specific techniques of resolving conflict are legitimately the topic of another book. The training of professional leaders requires the mastery of these techniques, for there are many who assert that this is the leader's most important role.

Awareness of progress. A fourth responsibility of the leader is to keep a record of what the group has done and what remains to be done. Small groups do not employ secretaries in the same way as do parliamentary meetings. A recorder-observer, if one is attached to the group, is as much concerned with interaction as he is with progress. It is the chairman who must be aware of agreements, disagreements, and unresolved issues in the group.

Where necessary, the leader summarizes what the group has agreed on and delimits the direction the discussion is to take from that point. To make transitions from one agenda item to another, the leader may review what has been decided in the previous step. Frequent summaries reinforce consensus. Members may be unaware that agreement has been reached, and may therefore raise necessary objections when the leader summarizes. If a member attempts to summarize, the leader will support him, so long as it does not appear that the member is attempting to arrogate the leadership role.

There are other responsibilities and duties of leadership that vary with the type of discussion. Those enumerated above are general requirements. In educational discussion, the leader must keep the group attentive to the topic. In therapeutic discussion, the leader must be prepared to interpret the behavior of members and feed the interpretations back at the appropriate time.

Styles of leadership

Whatever the discussion purpose, the leader behaves according to a style. His style sets the tone for the interpersonal activity of the group. There are four main styles:

The democratic leader functions as effective guide. The democratic style is preferred by most group members. The democratic leader attempts to guide rather than direct the group. In doing so, he leaves as many decisions as possible to the group.

A democratic leader need not take votes in order to create the façade of democracy. Rather, he conveys the impression that he is receptive to the ideas and desires of the group. When he summarizes or suggests, he does so in a permissive way, indicating that he is open to suggestions or objections. He does not let the group wander aimlessly, however, for his mastery of the agenda enables him to remind them about their responsibilities.

While most members respond positively to democratic leadership, occasionally groups will flounder when confronted with the necessity to make decisions. Students, particularly, are accustomed to a moderately directive style in the classroom. When faced with decisions, they may attempt to "pass the buck" back to the leader. It may be necessary for him to exert more control than he wanted to, in order to give his group a chance to learn democratic decision making. Leader and group alike should expect to make many mistakes while learning the process.

Democratic leadership is an effective compromise between the conflicting demands of efficiency and creativeness that are imposed on small groups. The style is fluid enough so that the leader can allow the group a maximum of digressions if it appears that creative ideas are resulting. It has enough discipline in it so that the leader retains the prerogative to bring the group back to the agenda when it appears they have strayed far from the point.

Permissive leadership encourages spontaneity. The permissive leader serves mostly as a central point around which communication can go on. He does not attempt to guide the group, though he may keep track of what it does and feed information back if called on to do so. This sort of leadership is well suited to creative activity. It is most useful in an educational milieu when any intervention by the teacher may be misconstrued as an attempt at direction stifling to the group.

If the ability of the group members varies widely, the permissive situation may result in domination by one or two people. When the group is made up of highly intelligent individuals with equal ability and motivation, they can usually be relied on to establish their own methods and restrictions. A leader would probably not be able to restrain them anyway, unless he imposed totalitarian control. The greatest service a permissive leader can render is to assume the role of recorder-observer. He should be ready to give information on request. He may also remind the group gently when they have wandered far afield. If the group must produce an outcome report or program, it may be necessary for the leader to become more directive in order to ensure achievement of the group goal.

Efficiency is the goal of authoritarian leadership. There are two principal ways in which authoritarian leadership can be displayed. The first is through the personality of the leader. The authoritarian personality wants to get things done, and usually in his way. His leadership consists of pushing the group in the direction he wants it to go. As long as he holds some external high status capable of affecting members of the group, he can be successful in securing verbal assent to his ideas. Members might even add valuable suggestions for implementation, even though they do not agree with the ideas at all. If he does not hold high status, he is likely to have a rebellion on his hands.

With groups not accustomed to the normal freedom of the discussion process, authoritarian leadership is sometimes indispensable, particularly in early stages of the discussion. In this case, however, the agenda can be the authoritarian, and the leader its means of enforcement. Once taken through the process via an authoritarian agenda, group members may be more responsive to democratic techniques, for they know how to do more for themselves.

A democratic leader can be temporarily authoritarian in order to expedite the group's goal. When group output is to be subjected to operations planning through PERT, the democratic leader must be sufficiently authoritarian that the final solution emerges in a form amenable to the technique.

The gradualness of the discussion process makes it unsuitable for decision making where immediate action is necessary. Some form of mild authoritarian control can preserve some of the benefits of the group method, yet avoid total control by the leader. For the most part, however, democratic leadership patterns are most compatible with discussion situations.

Leaderless discussion is a useful learning device. In discussion training groups it is sometimes beneficial to set up a situation where there is no designated leader. In so doing, various members will be motivated to assume leadership roles. Some will try to ensure compliance with an agenda. Others will summarize and offer critiques. Still others will try to act as referees in conflict situations. As each member assumes a leadership role, his understanding of the functions of leadership will increase.

Leaderless discussion helps prevent imposition of a hierarchical structure on the group. Each member feels an equal responsibility to play the role of leader and member. The group may generate its natural leaders. It may start by selecting a popular member to serve as leader during organizational phases. Later on, a more efficient, task-oriented leader can take over. Other types of leadership may emerge as necessary. Leaderless discussion is an excellent classroom technique, for group members can learn a great deal about the relationship of leader and group from it. The method forestalls initial appointment of incompetent leadership. Members will have a chance to observe each other in action before decisions about leadership must be made.

Sources of leadership

Leadership may become manifest in a group in a number of ways. The leader may hold an executive position in the organization to which the group is subsidiary. He may be appointed by an administrator. Once such a leader begins to work, his effectiveness is measured by how well he performs the functions expected of an effective leader. The organizational structure will endow him with enough respect to enable him to overcome initial objections. His position will prevent challenges to his leadership by subordinates.

Where the leader is not formally appointed, the first to emerge is usually the member who is most popular with the others. Although social acceptability may not seem to be a valid criterion for selection of a leader, it is a sign of general respect. It is essential that a leader enjoy some prestige in his group.

Personal popularity, however, is not enough to sustain leadership. The leader must either demonstrate skill at the process or display some special knowledge of the discussion topic if he is to continue to hold the respect and attention of the members. An individual who represents an unpopular point of view or displays a drastically different life style or set of values from that of most members usually is not accepted as a leader. Groups which are able to develop their own leadership tend to select members who represent an idealization of the opinion of the average member. The chosen leader will know somewhat more about the problem than the rest of the group, and his ideas on the question will conform to the thinking of most members.

Willingness is another essential for leadership. A member pressured into a leadership role may use an inappropriate style and disrupt the group. He may be permissive and lead the group into anarchy, or he may choose to be authoritarian to get the job over with as soon as possible. Leaders appointed by an administrative officer should be screened for assent beforehand. If the group chooses its own leader, it tacitly takes willingness into account. Sometimes it can overcome natural reluctance to lead by showing faith in the selected leader, demonstrating to him his importance to the accomplishment of the group's aims.

There has been much written on the topic of leadership, but there is still little evidence that it can be taught. The characteristics of effective leadership are somewhat hazy, and no clear image can be delineated of the personality type that would, infallibly, be an effective leader. Presumably, this would vary from group to group, depending on the composition of the membership and the assignment of the group. Skill with group processes can be taught, however, and we can accept as a basic premise that some ability to handle the duties of leadership is essential to success. Other necessary traits are controlled by the nature of the group and its personnel.

Interpersonal communication is the group's primary activity

Group members do their work by speaking and listening to each other. The pattern of communication is partly determined by the individual personalities of the group's membership. In turn, the pattern of communication exerts an influence on the behavior of members. Techniques of interpersonal communication will be discussed in Chapter Three.

A member who contributes a great deal becomes a focal point of communication. Group members interact with those who display a willingness to communicate. Persons who speak a great deal get spoken to a great deal. Having more than one talkative member in the group means that there will be a distribution of communications, even though they may revolve around various individuals.

If the leader talks a great deal, then contributions will be directed to him, and he may appear to be an authoritarian even though he did not elect to employ this style.

Communication patterns tend to be unequal. In any given group, there will be both talkative and silent members. It is rare that a group is composed of members who divide communications equally. At any event, quantity of output bears no necessary relation to quality of contribution to the group.

Status and acceptance in the group modifies direction of communication. Members with high status and acceptance in the group tend to initiate more communications than others. It is not entirely clear whether their status is a function of their communicative output or the reverse. It is obvious, however, that status and acceptance confer confidence. The member who does not feel that he is fully accepted by the group may restrain his output until he feels more secure. The high-status person can tolerate disagreement. Even if he expresses ideas contrary to those of the majority, his general acceptability will enable him to retain his position in the group. Some members may be concerned about his divergence and attempt to persuade him to alter his position. Some may be persuaded by him, since a minority opinion expressed by a highly acceptable member may make it seem worth believing.

When a group member does not feel secure, he will tend to withdraw and make only tentative moves toward communication. If he can identify high-status members, he may direct his remarks to them, hoping that if they accept him, others will follow suit. Once he feels integrated, the quantity of his communication may increase. If he desires to gain status for himself, he may attempt to identify others who seem rejected and direct his remarks to them. If they agree with him, a new cluster of power develops and either clashes with, or gains acceptance from, present leadership.

If a marginal member expresses an unacceptable opinion, other members may effectively isolate and ignore him rather than attempt to change his position.

Uniformity of opinion is achieved through communication. When members of a group are in unanimous agreement little needs to be said. Nods of affirmation are sufficient to signal concordance. When conflict or discord is present, communication among members must be increased in both quality and quantity in order to reach consensus. Consensus can be reached by one faction prevailing over another to accept an opinion. It can also be reached by isolating members who tend to disagree and persuading them one by one. Optimum consensus is reached by independent assent by each member.

Achieving consensus is the essential purpose of interpersonal communication. The group must first hear what ideas are available by encouraging maximum expression from members. The wider the range of attitude expressed, the better chance there is to develop an acceptable opinion capable of integrating all views. The deviant member need not always make concessions. High-status or accepted deviants can often change the "modal" or popular, attitude. It is only the socially unacceptable deviant that is rejected.

In large groups, members tend to direct their communications to persons similar to themselves. As a group gets larger, factions may begin to develop. Factions are clusters of members who confine their communications to others who believe as they do. Clusters may develop around criteria external to the discussion, such as race, religion, occupation, socio-economic values, and status.

Development of factionalism may lead to antagonisms. Cluster solidarity supersedes group solidarity. Until the factions can be persuaded to affiliate with the group goal, conflict potential between factions will be high and consensus blocked. When communications are restricted to persons of similar beliefs, attitudes harden. A faction can develop its own consensus and defend it against all comers, preventing consensus of the whole group.

The process of interpersonal communications can be understood as a game in which each player develops a set of rules for his own personal participation. The first step of the game consists of putting the private rules together into a public set of rules that can accommodate the larger number of members of the group. The next move is to utilize the group rules to "win" the game, that is, to achieve the group goal. Deviant players lose as individuals. Too many deviant players cost the group the possibility of achieving agreement and thus winning the game. Unanimous agreement on rules makes the game easy, and sometimes dull. Such agreement should be suspect, for it may mean that some members are suppressing their personal rules, temporarily, reserving the right to apply them later on as objections to the final agreement. Obstacles like objections, criticisms, or digressions give spice to the game, for the members must use their skill at interpersonal communication to overcome problems and achieve their goals.

Each group will thus take on a characteristic communication style. When a group has been together for a long time, they will tend to develop a kind of communicative shorthand which may mystify outsiders. When this happens, it becomes increasingly difficult to integrate new members into the group. It is too arduous for them to learn the rules, and the group will not be interested in adjusting itself to the personal rules of the new players. Such a group may tend to move away from reality in its decisions as it effectively blocks sources of new information and ideas.

Because individuals differ in their ideas and patterns of communication, each small group will be unique. The "same" group will show different communication patterns in each subsequent meeting, as one member, then another, assumes dominant roles. The excitement of the group process comes from this fact, that situations are never the same. Adaptability to ideas and fluidity in communication styles are basic attributes of effective group members.

Group size influences the style of operation of the group

The phrase "small group" has been used throughout this and similar books, but there is no clear agreement on the meaning of "small." One authority proposes a range from two to fifty members. Another specifies four to six members as the optimum small group. In general, members of the group should be able to speak directly to each other with minimum effort in order for it to qualify as "small." The size of the group has considerable influence on the manner in which it transacts its business.

Larger groups tend to develop subgroups with divergent goals. Any time there are more than two people involved in an activity, subgroups can appear. In a three-man group, two members can "gang up" on the third. Four-man groups can divide two-two and debate, or they can divide three-one. They may also fragment into units of one and be anarchic. Normally, however, if the group is small enough to permit direct communication, it is more likely to retain unity.

When a group must be subdivided to do various tasks, there will be a tendency of members to affiliate themselves with the tasks of the subgroup, thereby superseding their association with the main group goal. It appears to be easier to concur on a style when the group is very small. Sometimes conflicts can develop between subgroups which threaten the unity and purpose of the main group. In such cases, a method must be devised in the larger group to give adequate recognition to the work of the subgroup in much the same way as individual contributions are recognized in a smaller group.

Larger groups have more resources but diminish the role a member can play. The larger the group, the more likely it is that it will have members capable of doing necessary tasks. There may even be competition among members for choice assignments. Thus, expanding the size of the group tends to reduce the possible roles any individual can play and consequently reduces the opportunity for him to obtain status and recognition. Those members who do achieve status will be proportionately stronger, and the possibilities for splitting the group around two or three diverse personalities increase. It seems that groups tend to try to reduce themselves to manageable size, and therefore larger groups will be more likely to factionalize.

Organizations with a number of committees often notice that the committees become political forces that exert significant influences on the work of the main organization. A strong administration is needed to exert control over subgroups. Businesses demand this sort of coordination of various departments, lest one department achieve control over the others and seriously alter the operation of the company.

Larger organizations also have difficulty in providing recognition for individual contributions. In small, face-to-face groups, merely having a contribution accepted is sufficient reward. The warmth of acceptance can encourage reticent members to participate without much prodding by the leader or other members. In a large group, however, silent members tend to move to the fringes. Their potential contribution is lost, unless a way can be found to associate them with subgroups. This tends to bring about a paradoxical situation, for, as we have noted, the development of subgroups may mean disruption of the organization. For this reason, larger organizations, if they are to survive, develop rigid administrative controls over possible conflict between subgroups.

In smaller groups, administrative control is not so important. Leadership can be democratic. Various members can assume leadership roles from time to time without threatening the position of the functioning leader. Larger organizations must guard against usurpation of leadership and often build authoritarian or quasi-authoritarian administrative structures to do so.

The most effective group is small enough so that members can communicate face to face. One of the more fundamental notions about group discussion is that the process becomes unwieldy when the members can no longer sit around a table facing each other. As the size of the group increases it becomes more difficult to communicate, for voice level has to be raised and it is harder to look directly at the other members. If the group can be kept to a size where members can talk in normal conversational tones without expending much effort in trying to locate a respondent, the efficiency of the group is improved.

It is very difficult for conflict to remain below the surface in such a group. It comes to light quickly and can be dealt with, rather than remaining hidden and acting as a marginal or subliminal influence on individual behavior. It is harder for subgroups to split off from the face-to-face group. Consensus is easier to reach, for each member develops a responsibility to the group and feels a part of its decisions. Members of smaller groups find it easier to subordinate their personal agendas to those of such a group.

Research styles for investigation of the small group

The elements which affect the internal operation and output of groups have become the object of a growing body of research. In the main, interpersonal elements in the group have been studied, on the assumption that if interpersonal relations can be made optimum, the output of the group will be enhanced. Recently, however, some concern has been shown for discovery of specific techniques of improving output itself, and direct attempts have been made to discover the relationship between interpersonal processes and achievement of solution goals. In problem-solving groups, output is the main concern. Group interactions are important only as they can be shown to influence output. In educational and therapeutic groups, enriched interactions may lead to optimum conditions for learning and personal development.

One authority has commented that no social phenomenon has received more research attention in recent years than the small group.[1] Research efforts have followed diverse paths, based on a variety of theories. Some of the major approaches are described here, though not in detail. Those interested in further investigation of techniques and findings from each method should refer to the works listed in the footnotes. Additional materials are provided in the bibliography of this book.

Sociometry.[2] The sociometric approach to small-group study attempts to draw a visual diagram of the pattern of interpersonal affinities and rejections within the group. It is based on the assumption that groups composed of individuals who are favorably disposed toward each other will operate more effectively than those where individuals manifesting hostility are present. This technique has been widely employed in pedagogy, particularly for organization of task groups in the elementary classroom.

Sociometrists use a variety of observation methods, such as direct questioning, observation of interaction, and out-of-group observations of socialization and influence. From their observations they are able to discover concentrations of power, and rejected members.

[1] Robert Golembiewski, **The Small Group** (Chicago: The University of Chicago Press, 1962).
[2] See Jacob L. Moreno, "Foundations of Sociometry: An Introduction," **Sociometry,** IV (February 1941), 29. See also Jacob L. Moreno et al., **Sociometry Reader** (Glencoe: The Free Press, 1960).

They also purport to be able to construct optimum groups based on the most harmonious combination of persons.

The direct questionnaire, the basic tool of sociometry, asks members to indicate whom they enjoy working with, socializing with, whom they respect, whom they would prefer to avoid working with, who is their choice for leader, etc. The coded responses are then placed in an interaction matrix for analysis.

Another source of information for the sociometrist is observation of behavior. When studying a large group, for example, he may wish to discover the components of influential subgroups. It would be too difficult to ask direct questions, and therefore behavior is observed and then compared with hypothetical projections of influential combinations of members.

Sociometry is a useful method so long as excessive credence is not placed in the premise that interpersonal hostility always impairs the output of the group. Although conflict can be better managed if the members of the group are friendly to each other, it is questionable whether conflict will even arise in a group where all members are mutually acceptable. A hostile person acting as a gadfly is very helpful to the group. The main body of information from sociometric research is helpful in **ad hoc** studies of small groups in which the investigator attempts to explain what happened in the group in terms of the likes and dislikes of the members.

Interactionism.[3] The name "interactionism" was originally applied to work done by R. F. Bales in attempting to name and measure the types of oral contributions made by members of groups. The interactionist counts and classifies both verbal and nonverbal communications and then applies content analysis to the results in order to predict disunity, power struggles, and conflict between task and socio-emotional ideals. The interactionist tries to identify leaders of various kinds. A variant, "sign process analysis," professes to be able to measure the climate in small educational groups. It has the advantage of being able to delineate the flow of discussion in terms of positive, negative, and neutral contributions, but does not provide the depth of classification of the Bales system.

The basic assumptions of interactionist study are that the determinants of the discussion process are complex and should be appre-

[3]See Robert F. Bales, **Interaction Process Analysis: A Method for the Study of Small Groups** (Cambridge, Mass.: Addison-Wesley, 1950). See also Theodore Mills, **Group Transformations** (Englewood Cliffs: Prentice-Hall, 1964).

hended in some sort of complicated balance. Thus, they study a whole pattern of interactions rather than try to assess the influence of any one person. They are interested in patterns rather than individual contributions. Patterns of interaction can be compared between groups to discover essential differences.

Bales, for example, divides contributions into "task" and "socio-emotional" components. Task contributions are: "gives suggestion," "gives fact," "asks for fact," "asks for opinion," " asks for suggestion." Socio-emotional contributions are: "shows solidarity," "tension release," "agrees," "disagrees," "tension mounts," "shows aggressions." Each contribution, verbal or nonverbal, is classified under one of these headings. Analysis of the relationship of the total output of each member compared to the pattern for the group gives insight into the group climate and the influence of the individual members in building it. Attempts have been made to map direction of the contributions to co-ordinate with sociometric methodology, but the Bales system, so far, has been excessively complex for this type of study. The Mills system offers hope that classification and direction can be measured at the same time, though some sacrifice must be made of refined classifications.

One of the main deficiencies of the interactionist system of analysis is that it is very time-consuming to train observers to classify with reasonable consistency. Only after long months of training can observers agree on the classification into which communication acts should be put.

Mathematical models.[4] Some authorities have attempted to use mathematical techniques to derive an orderly system of hypotheses about the small group that could be tested experimentally. The method is based on attempts to formalize empirical observations into logical systems. One example is Heider's attempt to describe the balance between the relationship between people and the attitudes or sentiments expressed by them. Another experiment attempted to map the influence of a majority on decisions made by a minority. Generally, attempts have been made to formalize basic concepts of discussion such as leadership style or special social phenomena like interpersonal conflict.

[4]See Joseph Berger, Bernard Cohen, J. Laurie Snell, and Morris Zelditch, Jr., **Types of Formalization in Small Group Research** (Boston: Houghton Mifflin, 1962). For a description of a classic study, see Fritz Heider, **The Psychology of Interpersonal Relations** (New York: Wiley, 1958).

The influence of mathematical models on small-group research has been slight to date, because the vast number of variables in the discussion process seem to defy the precision of the symbolic logic and set theory that modelists have applied. Formalization of special theories has been usefully applied to group learning and retention of material in the group context.

Much of the work done by mathematical modelists is obscure to the lay student of small groups. Understanding of models requires both an understanding of group processes and mathematical theory. Research in the small group has been heavily influenced by statistical techniques, however, and many of the probability statistics applied to small groups have resulted from prior analysis by the mathematical model builders.

Game theory.[5] Mathematical game theory attempts to study interactions among members as predictable moves in a game. This type of formalization is often confusing when used to analyze a particular group, but is highly useful in simulating small-group interactions on the computer.[6] Such cybernetic analysis can help researchers determine the potentiality of responses that might occur if various personality types were placed in juxtaposition in diverse situations. While exact predictability is not possible because of the impossibility of obtaining either pure personality types or pure situations in real discussion, the use of simulation procedures is helpful in developing methods of observation of small groups and particularly in applying sociometric and interactionist data.

Psychiatric game theory, such as that developed in the transactional psychiatry of Eric Berne, is most useful in describing patterns of behavior in small groups. In Chapter Five we will apply this method to interpersonal relations in typical groups. Making analogies between verbal interchanges among members and moves in a game helps the researcher explicate and evaluate discussion situations, and, in addition, provides him with a method of interrupting disruptive interactions. Some interaction patterns approach neurosis and are detrimental to both member and group. The observer trained in game theory can assist the group by pointing out

[5]See R. D. Luce and H. Raiffa, **Games and Decisions** (New York: Wiley, 1957). See also Eric Berne, **The Structure and Dynamics of Organizations and Groups** (Philadelphia: Lippincott, 1963).
[6]G. M. Phillips, **GRPSEL: Computer Analysis of Group Interaction** (State College: Department of Speech, Pennsylvania State University, 1965).

the context and moves of these interaction games and suggesting alternate responses which might result in a healthier interaction pattern.

One caution should be kept in mind when studying psychiatric game theory—that is, it was developed for use with disturbed people. While it may explain a neurotic interaction, its application to the type of people usually encountered in small groups is questionable. The games played by "normals" are neither as rigid nor as destructive as the kinds observed by the psychiatrist. Care should be taken not to use the label "neurotic" loosely.

Phenomenological analysis.[7] Phenomenological analysis is a relatively new perspective, only recently applied to small groups. It is a useful way of getting a total impression of the activity of a group. Phenomenologically, the group is regarded as a total entity with a personality of its own, regardless of its "life history." What happens internally is not necessarily a summation or even a function of the activity of the members. The approach is a direct opposition to the approach of the sociometrist, interactionist, or mathematical modelist.

Phenomenological analysis stems from perception psychology and the existential approach to psychotherapy. Its application requires an understanding of the physiological, psychological, and sociological determinants of human behavior and how they become an amalgam in a group. The progression through various stages of skill in problem solving can be studied without reference to the causal contributions of members, except as those contributions become focal points of group activity. Group growth can be evaluated in a unique context, almost as a microcultural analysis with emphasis on the group's idiosyncratic problems and capabilities as well as its relation to external forces, and without any attempt necessary at separating internal parts. Study of individuals can take place after an assessment of the group style and personality has been made. Each member can also be analyzed phenomenologically once his social context is understood.

[7]There is no definitive work on phenomenological analysis of small groups. The closest approximation might be that by Mills, **Group Transformation**, referred to previously. Virtually any work detailing case histories of group operations might be partially phenomenological, inasmuch as the method is often used in combination with other methods in order to gain depth insight into the group personality.

The phenomenological approach emphasizes subjectivity in observation. It is based on the premise that attempts at objective study are rooted in the personalities of the observer and unless this is recognized such observation presents a distorted picture. The phenomenological approach permits a statement to be made about the unique qualities of a group, but groups cannot be compared except insofar as they are contiguous and act upon one another. That is, the phenomenological approach might increase understanding of one group, without necessarily offering information about groups in general.

A variant of the phenomenological approach is the **field-theory** approach,[8] in which the researcher attempts to develop a topological impression of the group on the premise that group outcomes are the result of vectors and valences of interaction. This means that the investigator views the group as a unique phenomenon (its topology), consisting of people who have attitudes (vectors) of various strengths (valences). This contradicts the so-called "dynamic" approach, where internal dynamics are regarded as determinants of individual behavior which in turn affects total group behavior.

Reference theory.[9] Reference theory is based on the principle that people's behavior in small groups is determined by their previous experiences. Such influences as family, remembrances of past successes and failures, the role of small groups in their subculture, educational experiences, and perception of self in the group are all influential. In addition, the fantasy, "What would I like to see happen in this group?" also affects behavior. Reference theory is Freudian in context as it attempts to determine the significance of the role of earlier influences on individual behavior.

While this method does not give solid information about the group as a totality, it offers many insights about the possible influences of ontological events on individual behavior in groups and helps the observer to hypothesize reasons for both positive and negative behaviors. Ontological events are occurrences that tend to cause the individual to come to be the way he is. Bradford's construct, "the hidden agenda," to be discussed in Chapter Five, came out of this approach to research.

[8]See Kurt Lewin, **Field Theory in Social Science** (New York: Harper, 1951).
[9]See Theodore Newcomb, **Personality and Social Change** (New York: Dryden Press, 1943). See also Musafer Sherif, **The Psychology of Social Norms** (New York: Harper, 1936).

Psychoanalytic.[10] The psychoanalytic approach to small-group study came primarily from the work of W. R. Bion in rehabilitation work in mental hospitals. Bion's work was done primarily with disturbed people and has been heavily conditioned by its need to account for neurotic behavior. Some of its principles are applicable, however, to understand normal group functions.

The fundamental premise of the theory is that the individual exposes his own personality as he functions in a small group. His covert personality tends to control some of his remarks, but he also attempts to adjust his manifest personality to the group culture. Certain personal needs can be satisfied or frustrated by the group culture, and the individual responds in such a way that he will maximize satisfaction and minimize frustration. To do this, he will form relationships with other group members which can only be understood in terms of satisfaction of personal needs.

A further premise of the theory, that of the need of people to come together in groups to have dependency needs satisfied by an individual, is more applicable to group therapy, in which the therapist disseminates "comfort" to group members and tends to hold the group together because of his position and ability to satisfy needs.

The idea of personality exposure is relevant to the study of small groups. Support for the idea has come recently from the work of anthropologists like Ernest Becker[11] who feel that the communication process represents an involvement of total personality, which in turn is the function of psychological, social, and physiological needs. On this point, psychoanalytic theory seems to blend with phenomenological analysis. Understanding of total personality would be useful in understanding the function of the whole group, and conversely, the group can be used as a matrix in which personality can be exposed and subjected to individual analysis.

Cognitive theory.[12] The cognitive approach to group interaction has become popular in current research, for it purports to explain interaction in terms of the communication process and the effects of units of communication on sender and receiver.

The theory is based on the idea that communication can be

[10]See W. R. Bion, "Experiences in Groups, I–VII," **Human Relations** (1948–1951).
[11]Ernest Becker, **The Birth and Death of Meaning** (New York: The Free Press, 1962).
[12]Leon Festinger, **A Theory of Cognitive Dissonance** (Evanston: Row, Peterson, 1957).

divided into units. As information is received, some units will be consistent or consonant with units already possessed, whereas others conflict, or are dissonant. Orientation to information can be explained by consonance or dissonance and responses can become more comprehensible to an observer.

The theory proposes methods for resolution of dissonance based on the observed tendency of a receiver of information to make information consonant. If there is an incongruity—e.g., an individual smokes but learns that smoking is injurious to health—he may resolve the incongruity by changing his mind about one of the units, or change a unit entirely, or bring in a third unit to resolve the dissonance. That is, he can decide not to smoke or that smoking is not injurious to health. He may also decide that air pollution is injurious to health and that smoking has little effect compared with that of pollution of the air. Finally, he can bring in information about the possibility of his developing a nervous disorder if he stops smoking.

An observer can classify behavior as "incongruous." To the behaver, however, no action is incongruous. Everything he does seems rational to him at the time he does it. This premise is supported by perceptual psychologists, who define "irrational behavior" as a product of the observer's classification system rather than an intrinsic state of a behaver. Understanding behavior from the perspective of the behaver is useful in explaining some of the basic problems attendant to interpersonal conflict in the small group.

Systems analysis.[13] Systems analysis is output-oriented. It is based on the belief that alteration in agenda or procedure of a group can alter quality of output. Setting up external requirements such as probabilities evaluation tends to commit the group to competition with externals rather than involve members in interpersonal contention with each other.

Systems methods utilize probability theory to give the group an appraisal of its chances of achieving a specified goal. In order to apply the probability test, the solution must be phrased in such a way that program activities and goals are obvious. The operation procedure must be planned in detail, complete with assessment of

[13]See Mary Arnold, John Hess, and James Bemis, eds., **Health Program Implementation,** to be published in 1966 by Western Branch, American Public Health Association, for a discussion of the application of systems-analysis procedures.

resources, deployment of personnel, and computation of times for operations. Time is the constant used for the probability analysis. This method will be explained in detail in Chapter Four.

While systems theory appears to be rigid, it is highly effective when used by problem-solving groups. It assists a group in formalizing their activities without sacrificing the democratic atmosphere of the group. It provides an automatic agenda of formal rules that helps the group to assess its progress toward its goal. Existence of rules tends to make members more co-operative with each other; their competition is with the requirements of the agenda system.

In subsequent chapters we will deal with discussion in education and therapy and techniques of problem-solving discussion. We will also discuss interpersonal relations among group members. The discussions will be heavily influenced by the writer's bias toward game theory and systems analysis.

The small group in education and therapy

The small group in education

Small-group methods have been extensively used in a number of educational contexts. Building on the pioneer work of John Dewey, educators discovered that there was much to be gained by supplementing the formalized lecture and recitation system by encouraging greater participation by students in the learning process. The interpersonal benefits to be gained by interacting with peers, they found, far outweighed the possible loss of authority in the classroom. Despite the limitations, however, it was discovered that discussion can be generally used in learning situations where appreciation of concepts or ability to apply complex material is the goal.

The classroom teacher has many roles. He is a source of facts with whom the students interact orally to learn material which books may not make adequately clear. The kindergartner confronts education for the first time in an oral context. It is through verbal persuasion and prodding that he is guided to sufficient skill in mastery of reading, on which his subsequent training depends.

The teacher also motivates the student to undertake more complex material by dramatizing the quest for knowledge and making it real and alive. In addition to this, the teacher often serves as a surrogate parent or authority for the student, who develops varying degrees of dependency on him. The student identifies with his teacher, receives support from him, learns the values of his society, and often seeks advice and counsel from this, a most influential figure in his life. Because of the possibility of excessive dependency of student on teacher, some variation of the authoritarian tone of the classroom seemed necessary.

Initial objections to the general use of the discussion method in the classroom were twofold. First, discussion takes more time and is considerably less efficient than more formal pedagogical procedures. Second, it is hard to draw definitive information on which students can be tested out of the interpersonal processes of discussion.

Nevertheless, so much of the teacher's contact with his students takes the form of verbal interaction that it is wholly natural for him to expand his classroom role by establishing a live discussion format to dilute some of the transference and dependency the student has on him and make the student more able to make independent decisions. "Transference" refers to the process of one person developing a relationship to another, based on the past relationship of the former with his parents, teachers, or friends. The attitude held in the past is "transferred" so that the teacher may be regarded by a student as a father or friend, rather than in his correct role. It is worth the sacrifice of efficiency to accomplish the full growth of the student, instead of perennial concentration on mastery of subject matter in a teacher-centered classroom.

The discussion method supports the general goals of teaching. Through discussion, the teacher can make subject matter alive for the student by confronting him with problems and situations that require personal effort to resolve. Discussion gives the student greater responsibility for learning. Additionally, it trains him to play a more effective role in his society, where interaction in small groups is so important. The typical classroom is directed to the convenience of the teacher as he directs the students in mastery of material. The teacher's goals may not necessarily accord with those of the student. To do a more effective job of teaching it is necessary for the teacher to discover what the student wants to gain from his learning and find ways in which subject matter can be made more meaningful in terms of student-centered needs.

The hope of every teacher is to be able, eventually, to bring the student to the point where he no longer needs guidance in order to learn. It is not possible to do this while students are passive and inert recipients of information dispensed by an omniscient teacher. Only when the student is left to his own devices and permitted the freedom to make errors can he learn his own techniques of problem solving and develop his own style of discovery of learning.

The discussion method is not a panacea for all the problems that exist in the classroom. Nevertheless, a flexible teacher, able to shift, where necessary, from lecture-recitation to discussion can facilitate learning for the students by application of an appropriate method to the demands of the material he teaches. The discussion method is not well suited to the teaching of factual material. It must be assumed that before the students participate in small-group activities they will have acquired substantive knowledge from both teacher and books. There is no danger that discussion will replace traditional methods entirely. Just the reverse seems to be the case. The discussion method is an excellent device for motivating students to bend more effort to their textbook studies and to pay more attention to the teacher's lectures in order to acquire the information they need to be effective in the group discussion.

The teacher who is competent in motivating students to learn from him and from books is well equipped to introduce the discussion method into the classroom. Certain theoretical concepts must be understood before the attempt is made.

1. Goals and limits must be clearly marked for students prior to the start of discussion. The student must not regard the classroom discussion as a signal for anarchy. If the teacher can establish clear rules of procedure before he withdraws to permit the students to try their hand, then they can behave within the limits of their delimited authority without in any way jeopardizing the position of the teacher as the central authority in the classroom. The teacher must, of course, take into account the background of the students. Taking students who have experienced only authoritarian environments in learning and placing them in the relative democracy of discussion often results in unpleasant situations. It is not inappropriate for the teacher to offer some training in discussion method before attempting to use it with classroom material. Without such training, classroom discussions rarely rise above the level of stereotyped responses to oral reports—considerably duller than even the dullest of the teacher's lectures.

2. The teacher seeks to bring the student to the point where he can accept responsibility for his own growth as a human being. To accomplish this, the student must be allowed to react in situations where his errors will be sanction-free. The teacher cannot use discussion as a stratagem for punishment of weaknesses. Rather, mistakes must be remarked clearly and calmly outside the discussion framework. It is even more effective if the student-discussants can mature to the point where they can discover mistakes so that peer criticism within the group can provide a remedial milieu for understanding of material under discussion. That behavior that pertains to the discussion method cannot be punished at all. The student must be unhampered in his efforts to find a way to relate to his colleagues in the discussion context.

3. In order to make the discussion work, there must be a harmonious relationship between the students and teacher. Discussion cannot remedy a defective rapport in the classroom; it can reinforce such positive rapport as already exists. The teacher must make it clear, before initiating discussion, that questions, comments, and arguments are welcome. The teacher cannot show that he is personally threatened when students object to his ideas, for once the discussion is underway it is likely that most of the teacher's pet notions will be challenged. In this way the students test the teacher's orientation to a student-centered environment. If the teacher shows any tendency to penalize students for the ideas they present, no matter how outlandish they may be, they will quickly get the idea that the purpose of the discussion is to ratify the teacher's convictions rather than learn their own, and the discipline will revert back to authoritarianism. For this reason, it is usually not wise for the teacher to enter into the discussion himself. In so doing, there are two possible perils. First, the students might be perceptibly influenced by the teacher's authority. Second, the teacher may lose authority in other contexts, because the students begin to regard him as a peer.

4. The discussion method cannot be used in isolation as an end in itself. It must be carefully integrated into the subject matter of the course and used only on material suitable to it. Discussion in the classroom must be accompanied by discussion about the discussion. It must be evaluated, analyzed, and summarized by a teacher who has functioned as a careful observer-recorder rather than as a corrective authority. It must be harmonized with other subject mat-

ter. Objective testing is not appropriate for material covered in a discussion context. Testing must discover whether the student has broadened his range of expression and appreciation of ideas. If the student gets the idea that the objective of discussion is rote learning of specific subject matter, the whole purpose will be defeated.

5. The teacher must be flexible, able to stop and start discussion where necessary and motivated. Formal announcement that "there will be a discussion of this material during the next class period" impedes rather than assists the discussion process. Spontaneity is the best motivation to effective student discussion.

6. The teacher must recognize the human potential of each student, and believe that there is a latency for worthwhile contribution from each student. If this is not communicated clearly, the discussion will be dominated by those who feel most secure with the teacher. Others will withdraw from participation or serve only as echoes of material they think is acceptable to the authority in the classroom.

Keeping the above cautions in mind, discussion is applicable to virtually all levels of education. The success of such maligned techniques as "show and tell" and "sharing" indicates that students want to interact at a very early age. If a student's training in communication begins with discussions very early in elementary school and continues throughout, it is entirely likely that by the time he reaches college he will be able to assume the role of independent scholar and accept his responsibilities in the academic milieu.

The small group in therapy

Small-group therapy is one of the most widely used rehabilitation procedures applied to a broad spectrum of human problems. It is extensively used both in mental hospitals and in private psychiatric and psychological practice, for the treatment of mental, social, and personality disorders. The assumption of group therapy, wherever it is used, is that interaction with peers and/or re-creation of family structure can be supportive and encouraging to the subjects of therapy. A commonly held premise is that people with problems feel better when they understand that they are not the only ones to suffer from their disorder.

In addition to psychological problems to which group therapy has been applied, it has also been used to treat psychosomatic disorders, allergies, drug addiction, alcoholism, and various pathologies of speech (especially stuttering), as well as for rehabilitation of geriatric patients, training of women in the techniques of motherhood, and rehabilitation of unwed mothers. In social areas, it has been applied to delinquency, penal correction, child guidance, and family services, as well as in counseling about sex and marriage problems. The group approach has been widely used to disseminate information about family planning and community mental health and most recently has been applied to industrial training and accident prevention. For the most part, the real strength of group therapy lies in prevention rather than cure. It is most useful with people who have not descended too far into their problem, or with those who recognize the need for cure and are internally motivated to change their behavior.

The basic difference between the group used in a therapy context and more traditional groups in problem solving and education is that in the latter, the individual tends to subordinate his personal goals to those of the group. The member becomes part of a totality, and temporarily surrenders part of his identity as he interacts with others to achieve a common goal, either a solution or an understanding. In a therapy group, the patient remains an individual, for in reality there is no group goal. The object of therapy is to bring about intrapsychic changes in the patient: to revise some attitude or inculcate a behavior change. It is difficult, if not impossible, for the patient in a therapy group to give up his identity to the group, although he must learn to respond to his fellow members. It is the reinforcement of identity through interaction that induces personal change, whereas in other types of discussion, interaction influences group consensus. The identity of the member of a therapy group is presumably so severely threatened that he needs help to discover himself. Immersion in a group would be injurious to his self-esteem. For this reason, no common goal is stipulated in the therapy group.

While the therapist does not actively direct his group in its activities, he is the essential center around which interaction flows. The relationships which emerge between the various members of the therapy group are incidental to the relationship between the individual members and their therapist.

The inherent strength of group therapy comes from the information that the therapist gleans from the interactions, as well as insights gained by the patient from feedback about his behavior in the form of response from the group and comment from the therapist. Therapy subjects may learn new methods of behavior, particularly techniques of verbal interaction designed to eliminate or minimize the situational ploys and activities that gave rise to the tensions leading to the disturbance. Throughout, the therapist plays a central role, and those aspects of transference which influence any individual therapy relationship are of equal importance in group therapy. The therapist must not only consider the range and valence of interactions among the members of the group but must also interpret the attitudes and responses directed to him by the group members.

Basic approaches to group therapy

The traditional lecture forum. A lecture-type format is often used by therapists for those adjustment problems in which dissemination of information is essential. Briefing sessions at the time of admission to an institution or conveying instructions about group or occupational therapy are illustrations of such situations. Basic information is presented to groups of patients via a speech. Then a type of forum is employed so that patients can raise pertinent questions. To enhance question-asking, the main group is split into small groups of three or four to prepare lists of questions for the therapist-lecturer. Questions can either be presented anonymously or in the form of reports by a spokesman for each of the small groups.

Discussion therapy. More widely used is a therapy which employs both the format and procedures of the traditional group-discussion approach. The emphasis, however, is not on consensus or subject-matter mastery, but on the interpersonal dynamics of the group members. The therapist is not so much concerned with what the group does or decides as a totality, as he is with what the group does to the behavior of each member. This is analogous to the differences between lecture-recitation in the classroom, where the focus of the teacher is on subject matter or drill, and the group method, where the concern is for active participation in learning. The therapy-group member learns individually, and there is no precise goal for him to achieve established by the therapist. Private goals emerge from the interaction and are encouraged or discouraged by the therapist as he evaluates their possible use in rehabilitation.

The requirements of the effective therapy group are based on traditional Freudian concepts. Group therapy must be preceded by a careful taking of the history of each patient and careful observation of the patient in a natural setting so that the therapist has a clear picture of what constitutes normal behavior for the individual. The therapy group must be constructed with care to minimize the potential for severe threat transmitted from patient to patient. This does not mean that all potential threat must be removed from the group. It is important that controversy and clash take place so that the therapist can observe the patient's response to interpersonal tension, and so that the patient can learn some skills in responding to hostile situations.

A second requirement of discussion-based therapy is that a relationship develop between the patients and the therapist. Psychoanalytic methods of free association or individual storytelling are often employed to explicate relationships. Each patient acts as an individual to reveal something of his character and personality. Members are free to discuss what has taken place, and relationships between patients develop from this discussion. The therapist exerts minimal control of interaction, for it is essential that the patients not think of him as an authoritarian. Permissiveness and nondirection are essential, for the therapist initially enters the group with the status of "healer." It is imperative that the patients lose sight of his halo of authority if maximum information is to be derived from interactions between group members. If members behave to please the therapist, then their natural state of behavior cannot be analyzed.

In final phases of group therapy some attempt may be made to systematize interactions so that the group receives some training in structure and development of group mores. This type of therapy closely approximates problem-solving discussion. Patients are confronted with tasks they must work out together. Hopefully, if rehabilitation has taken place at all, they will be able to move toward the normal state of group discussion, in which they are able to distinguish between their personal desires and the essential requirements of the group.

Semantitherapy. A widely employed therapeutic device is based on general-semantics systems. The goal of this kind of therapy is rehabilitation of language behavior, particularly where the patient has incorrectly evaluated his difficulty. Understanding the possible pitfalls of language assists the patient in making a more adequate assessment of self. Those who use semantitherapy employ the group method to teach the basic principles of general semantics to show the patient how to distinguish among statements of fact, inference, and value and to understand the abstraction process and its influence on human behavior.

Formats for educational and therapeutic discussion

The group process is so extensively applied that no single format can be called typical. The standard agenda is commonly used in problem-solving discussion. It will be discussed in detail in the next chapter. Use of this relatively restrictive format is not necessarily helpful, however, in discussion applied to education or therapy. Various approaches may be used to fit the requirements of group goals. Many can be used to fit the processes of both educational and therapeutic discussion, even though their goals are quite different. There is, of course, nothing to prevent problem-solving discussion groups from employing special techniques as well, provided that they are motivated by events in the discussion and that all the members are willing to digress from the agenda. It is up to the group leader to determine when direct problem solving might be aided by the application of a special technique. The emphasis to be placed on discussion method depends on the group and their desired output. Role playing, for example, can be used in problem solving to help resolve conflict, in educational discussion to clarify complicated ideas, and in therapy as a projective device. The group must determine what they want to derive from a method.

Brainstorming. One of the charges leveled by critics against the discussion process is that it stifles creativity. A member who gets good ideas rapidly may be at a loss in a group situation where he must adjust to the pace set by the other members. The format known as "brainstorming" permits group members to make contributions as rapidly as they occur to them. No flight of fancy is barred. No creative contribution is prohibited. As each comment is made, no critical threat is posed to the contributor. Customarily, in brainstorming, the group sits around a tape recorder. They have usually completed a preliminary investigation of their problem and may either be trying to understand causes of a situation (as they might in educational discussion), proposing behavior changes (as they might in a therapeutic discussion), or proposing solutions (as they might in problem solving).

The discussion leader opens by restating the problem clearly and succinctly. Each member can then say anything that occurs to him, as it occurs to him. He can elaborate on someone else's comments or present original ideas. His remarks are not even controlled by the criterion of relevancy. Contributions are made rapidly with no necessary order. The leader may direct traffic flow if several members try to speak at the same time. Comments are necessarily brief, but there is no limit to the number of contributions made by each member. The brainstorming is continued for a short time, usually about fifteen minutes, after which the tape is played back and the group evaluates the ideas to select those with potential for further exploration.

The problem census. Sometimes groups reach an impasse where it seems that they will never be able to reach agreement even on minor points. Although it would be easy to resolve problems by voting, such a procedure tends to factionalize the group. Instead, the members may be asked to re-examine their opinions to clarify sources of disagreement and discover areas of agreement. The chairman initiates discussion by reviewing the question that is troubling the group. Each member, in turn, expresses his attitudes briefly without comment from others. The chairman then attempts to synthesize agreements and disagreements from the comments. A summary statement is made as a basis for another effort to find a working consensus.

Role playing. A technique applicable to all forms of discussion is role playing, sometimes referred to as psychodrama or sociodrama. Group members improvise dramatizations of situations analogous to the problem the group is working on. In acting out situations, members reveal their conflicts, wishes, fears, attitudes, and daydreams. Used in problem solving, role playing is quite helpful in delineating differences that separate variant points of view. In a dispute, for example, involving the divergent goals of labor and management, each contending party may gain a clearer understanding of what motivates the other side. Having gained this understanding, both sides can proceed more empathetically toward agreement.

In educational discussion, members may be assigned roles in advance and be given an opportunity to do some research. For example, if the class is studying the relationship between control of public education and the political structure of the community, role players can be assigned to act variously as school superintendent, board president, principal, or representatives of various community pressure groups. A problem can be presented to the group, and each member acts out the views and attitudes of his role. Observers are enabled to gain insight into the way the issues of the problem affect the various factions involved. Role playing as sociodrama sometimes employs professional actors to dramatize a social problem for community audiences, which are then resolved into small groups for discussion of the performance they have seen.

In psychotherapy, role playing as psychodrama is used primarily to enable the therapist to understand the feelings and hostilities of the patient in a behavioral context. While it might be impossible, for example, for a psychotherapist to observe the relation between a disturbed child and his mother in a natural setting, it is possible for the child to act out a role in which he plays himself, with another person representing the mother. He may also switch roles and act out his mother's role as he perceives it.

Wherever used, role playing must be followed by an analysis and evaluation session, so that conclusions can be drawn. It cannot be used without fitting it into a problem context. Role playing is difficult to motivate and works only if members are willing to submerge themselves in their roles. Even employing normal people in an educational or problem-solving context, delicate and potentially disturbing personality issues can arise that might result in subsequent interpersonal difficulties. For this reason, the technique should only be used by those who are well trained in its potential and consequences. Role playing is a specialized device and should not be relied on to do what can be done by an effective group leader. Normally, it should be used only as a last resort in problem solving. In education it should not be employed unless the teacher is sure of the theoretical potential of his group. In therapy it should rest in the hands of a well-trained therapist.

The case method. The case method is a valuable educational tool and of considerable worth in initiating problem solving. The process opens when the leader presents a written narrative of a case or problem to the group. The case is selected to illustrate major ideas that the group will cover in ensuing discussion. The members participate in a nondirected analysis of the case.

Sometimes members will focus their attention on human relationships in the case, sometimes on the issues illustrated. A case selected that is similar to the group's problem will help it get an idea of the information it needs to do an effective job of discussion. It will also preview the issues and conflict points they are likely to encounter.

In the classroom, the case method makes it possible for the teacher to direct the student's deliberations to an issue illustrative of theoretical or factual material they have learned. The case method seems to work best in the social sciences, particularly political science and sociology. Some attempts at use of the case method have been made in clinical psychology, where the counselor presents his clients with a case similar to their own problem. In commenting on the case, the client may gain an understanding of his own perplexity so that he can discuss it more clearly with his counselor.

The buzz session. At large meetings, workshops, and conventions, it is often desirable to get members working together in smaller groups. It has been noted previously that the lecture approach to group therapy utilizes the small group in association with formal speaking to generate questions for the therapist.

The technique known as the "buzz session" can be employed to develop small groups out of a larger body. Customarily, a speaker presents a lecture to a large group. The group is then split into small groups of four to six which may remain seated on the auditorium floor or move off to predetermined meeting places. Each group is assigned to discuss the content of the lecture and prepare a response to it. Sometimes the groups are required to answer a problem question, to name a spokesman, and to report their findings publicly to the main group. The reports provide a sort of consensus of attitudes and understanding on the subject. If the speaker is to continue his lecture, he can proceed on the basis of the feedback he has received.

A modification of the buzz session is often used as a project technique in workshops. The subject matter may be presented in lecture or written form. Project problems are presented to subgroups, which may have up to a full day to work out their solution. Resource experts are usually available for consultation with the small groups.

Observer feedback. Observer feedback is a corrective device employed by groups to generate critical comments about member behavior during discussion. A well-trained observer with no stake in the group outcome is designated. His job is to evaluate the participation of each of the members as well as that of the group as a whole. Sometimes he may be called upon to keep a record of agreements, decisions, and problems confronting the group. He looks for friction points, reasons for conflict, problem interactions, inadequacies in information, etc. At stipulated intervals, or when the group seems to be in trouble, the observer is called on to report. He may add his suggestions for improvement, but mainly his report is a factual statement of what he has observed. The members should have the privilege of deciding how they wish to respond to the information the observer has given them. Correctives suggested by members are more acceptable and helpful than directives from the observer.

The observer-recorder is an excellent pedagogical device, for it enables group members to get a dispassionate view of themselves seen from outside the heat of discussion. Classroom teachers, however, must guard against a tendency to give directive criticism. Maximum leeway should be given the group to respond with its own ideas for improvement. The members must not get the impression that there is only one "right" way to proceed. It goes without saying that the observer must be skilled in the discussion process, understand the potential for interaction in small groups, and have considerable knowledge about the question being discussed.

Restatement. Discussion may bog down because some members do not understand what others are talking about. Their responses may be distorted by their biases, or else some of the ideas presented may be excessively complicated. An effective antidote to this communication barrier is to require, for a short period of time, that each person who responds to a remark must first summarize his understanding of it to the satisfaction of the person who made it.

When this procedure is initiated in a group, members are often shocked by the discrepancy between what they thought they heard and what the speaker thought he said. Sometimes restatement helps the original contributor to modify his own remarks. It may also make the listener more able to grasp the meaning of the comment he heard. Clarification of this sort does much to prevent the possibility of conflict about issues that are not real.

Expert testimony and joint research. When a group lacks information there are two efficient ways to get it. The first is to utilize the talents of experts. The group decides what information it needs and prepares a list of questions. A competent expert is invited to visit the group and answer questions. His responses may suggest new questions as well as untapped information sources. If differing perspectives on a problem are needed, a panel of experts can be invited to discuss the problem from their varying points of view.

A second approach to gathering of information is to resolve the group as a task group around a new discussion question, "What would be the best method for us to use in gathering information about our problem?" The group prepares an operation plan for research and divides up the work. If the various members complete their assignments, the group is assured of a sufficiency of facts.

Although it is necessary that a participant in discussion be well prepared, it is not always reliable for the group to depend on individual preparation. Groups should be prepared to use the joint-investigation method when it becomes obvious that members cannot contribute sufficient information. Further, if individual members are encouraged to prepare complete, individual studies of the problem, there is always the possibility that some of them will develop commitments to various ideas and in their defense of them will resist cooperation in arriving at consensus.

Public discussion. The discussion format can be used for large meetings in lieu of a public address. While this type of discussion does not entirely meet the criteria for small-group activity, it affords an opportunity to present material to an audience in an exciting and lively group format. The "University of Chicago Round Table" is an example of such public discussion.

The purpose of public discussion is not to solve problems or to arrive at consensus, but rather to dramatize ideas for an audience. The most popular formats are the panel and the symposium. The panel consists of a group of three or four experts who carry on a public conversation about a topic. The leader functions only to break up disputes and decides who speaks next. He does not seek to bring about agreement among panel members, but at the conclusion of the discussion he attempts to summarize the ideas presented.

The symposium is a more formalized approach. The members of a symposium are selected as representatives of differing positions on an issue. Each member delivers a short speech summing up his attitude. The speakers are then permitted to question each other and carry on a panel discussion. Sometimes the audience is invited to participate in a forum after the formal presentation.

A variant approach is the joint-interview technique exemplified by such popular television programs as "Meet the Press" and "Face the Nation." In this format, a group of well-trained interrogators cross-examine an expert and attempt to draw from him the implications of his ideas about current, vital issues.

Though the techniques of speaking in public discussion differ somewhat from those in discussion, the formats are so similar that an understanding of one assists more effective participation in the other.

Techniques of communication in the small group

A member of a small group does not occupy a position of advocacy. In theory, at least, he does not seek to dominate the group or persuade its members. His goal is participation with others to achieve a common goal. Direct clash, characteristic of debate, or overt persuasive appeals may incline the group to conflict inimical to its goal. Effective communication in small groups calls for a speaking style somewhat different from that of the public platform or the lecture hall.

The small-group member has understanding as the goal of his speaking and listening. It is impossible to arrive at consensus unless each member understands what the others are talking about. For this reason, the speaker in a small group will strive to avoid partisan, persuasive, and emotion-laden statements. He will not attempt to overpower the group with his erudition or zeal but will express his ideas clearly so they can be easily understood with minimal effort by his listeners.

To avoid sounding like a verbal duelist, challenging others to combat, the discussant adopts a moderate voice and tone. A normal, conversational demeanor is the most potent style for a small group.

Antagonisms between people can develop because of response to tone of voice as easily as they can from clash of ideas. It is not difficult to stir up unnecessary tension in discussion without attacking ideas directly. The close proximity of participants to each other makes them hypersensitive to the mannerisms of their associates. The muttered comment, facial grimace, or intolerant posture, relatively harmless to a platform speaker, can be most disconcerting to a speaker in a discussion group. The members of the group cannot be regarded as an "abstract audience." They must be considered as associates, partners, who will respond almost with hair-trigger rapidity to messages sent their way. At no time can members allow themselves to lose sight of their fellows as joint participants in a co-operative inquiry.

Since advocacy is not a goal, ideas should not be attacked. It is most helpful to the group if opposing sentiments can be expressed as questions rather than as frontal assaults. All members should be allowed the right of self-expression without feeling hidden threats. Sooner or later, if the discussion is to succeed, differences will have to be reconciled. For this reason, it is better to disagree as quietly as possible. This does not mean that potential critics must swallow their remarks and seek spurious harmony. It does mean that care must be taken to be sure of points of difference before critical remarks are made. Careful listening and calm questioning will permit members to separate out what they agree on before undertaking a consideration of differences.

A direct assault on a member will usually elicit a response in kind. The member who presented the idea will feel compelled to defend his opinion and himself. If questions are asked first to discover the meaning and implications of ideas, both speaker and critic can work together to fashion a statement at least partially acceptable to both before they begin to consider their areas of disagreement.

Individual members must also seek to avoid an aura of social dominance because of their participation. The group is not necessarily assisted by a great deal of talk. As a matter of fact, some groups are severely hampered because one person seeks to talk more than is reasonable. Those not as volatile and effusive will feel frustrated, then hostile, if they are denied the opportunity to speak. Avoiding egocentrism and adopting humility will help the talkative member to reduce his output somewhat. Because discussion is a co-operative effort, no member ought to be so vain as to assume that his comments are always more valuable than anyone else's.

The normally quiet person must recognize, also, that he has an obligation to present his ideas to the group. The group decisions are the result of the interaction of all of the members. The quiet person should not be overly self-critical as he evaluates his own ideas. They should be presented to the group for evaluation. It is not wise for him to sit back and decide that his remarks would not be worthwhile. That is a decision legitimately made by the group. In avoiding presentation of ideas, he may be denying the group important information or cogent opinion.

Of course, group members must attempt to stay on the subject. Digressions, while not particularly serious in themselves, serve to lengthen the group process. If each member is careful to direct his remarks with precision to the phase of the subject presently being considered, the progress of the group is expedited.

Good listening is vital to successful communication in discussion. The good listener will attempt to understand remarks in the context in which they are made. He will not jump to conclusions about what another member means. He will wait, instead, until the speaker is done, and if he feels hostility he will attempt to find out whether conflict is necessary by sensitive and intelligent questioning. Members should also be alert to nonverbal behavior of their colleagues. Facial expressions, hand gestures, nods of the head, and body motions communicate significant cues which, if responded to, would be very useful in understanding the feelings of other members. Often the shy, quiet person will try to express his opinions in the form of nonverbal cues. Response to these makes him feel more a part of the group and brings about his support for the consensus.

Above all, clarity in speaking should be sought. The skills required of the extemporaneous speaker can be applied to speaking in discussion. The ability to organize material rapidly and relevantly and to present it in a unified structure helps maximize understanding and cooperation. Statements should not be disjointed and cryptic. The discussion speaker must still present a unified whole with introduction, body, and conclusion, though in capsule form. The improvisation of coherent discussion contributions demands a great deal of skill and practice, but once achieved it is the group member's most valuable asset.

Sources of trouble in communication in small groups

There are several problems that seem to arise consistently to trouble
the verbal interaction in small groups. Observance of a few simple
cautions about communication helps members to avoid them.

1. It is not prudent to assume that each individual uses words
precisely the same way. A serious problem in interpersonal communication arises from the assumption that words mean exactly the same
thing to everyone. Phrases like "private enterprise," "the American
way of life," "morality," or "virtue" can be defined in many ways. To
understand what the speaker means it is necessary to question him
carefully and seek answers that refer to things that can be observed,
rather than abstractions and generalities. Contradicting a member
prematurely leads to unnecessary hostility. It may well be that there
is no real issue. This cannot be ascertained until vague words are
made concrete. Then, if a dispute is necessary, it can revolve around
real disagreements. Discord about vague representations is almost
impossible to quell. Understanding based on specifics helps to prevent this unnecessary disturbance of group progress.

2. Disproportionate involvement of personality in communication
is dangerous. There is a tendency for us all to assume that someone
else's ideas are invalid if they are not similar to our own. This attitude must be discarded in a discussion. Members must recognize
that each comes from a different environment and background, and
as a result their points of view on problems will be somewhat different. Agreement is possible, however, because, in general, there are
more similarities among people's ideas than differences. If the temptation to spontaneous criticism of apparently divergent ideas can be
suppressed, then it is possible to discover similarities first. Usually
the main point of a contribution demonstrates that opinions are
pretty much the same even though they have been derived from
different sources and for different reasons.

3. There is a tendency, particularly in problem-solving discussions
to jump to a consideration of conclusions before a thorough analysis
has been made of the problem. Questions often seem transparently
clear at the outset, only to have subsequent investigation reveal their
complexity. A group can arrive at an unworkable solution if they are
premature about their agreement on solutions. The desire to suggest
conclusions should be resisted until it is obvious that the entire

group is ready to move on. There should be sufficient information available to enable solutions to be satisfactorily evaluated. This should not occur until the group has made a thorough examination of facts and causes and has taken a good look at itself in order to discover its capability to solve the problem. This material will be discussed in detail in the next chapter.

4. Overformalization of process frequently subverts the value of the discussion process. Most people have had perfunctory experience with formal parliamentary procedure, and there is a natural tendency to attempt to apply those rules to discussion. Such formalization impedes spontaneous and direct contact between members. Conversation in discussion should be face to face without impediment. Remarks need not be addressed to the chairman, unless of course he is the object of the remark. The group should not have to resort to "points of order" and "points of information." Members may comment about procedure, make suggestions for improvement, and ask questions directly. The response to straightforward communication is usually equally straightforward. The parliamentary format is better suited to debate over adoption of a single proposition. Overly formal procedure tends to polarize the group and stir up conflict instead of co-operation.

This does not mean, however, that the group can afford to be disorderly about agenda. Structure in the order in which ideas are discussed makes discussion more efficient and effective. It is formalization in communication behavior that impedes direct contact that must be avoided.

5. Emotional problems disrupt discussion. People often clash because they perceive threats to their needs and values. Part of this comes from their inability to distinguish between statements of belief and statements of fact. Evaluations like "Jones is a good governor" are not facts, no matter how factual they appear, and hence they can stir up considerable controversy. If each member displays some concern about distinguishing between facts and values, much personal threat can be avoided. For example, in response to the statement about Governor Jones, the appropriate approach is a question designed to elicit information about things he has done. It is much easier to gain agreement on factual statements than about beliefs or attitudes. If each statement of belief can be traced back to the facts which led to its genesis, consensus is made easier.

It is unwise to stigmatize or label other members. Name calling can only hinder the discussion process. Generally, members should avoid evaluative statements, particularly those about other people. Critical comment should be confined to ideas expressed rather than behavior of the person who expressed them. It is equally unwise to presume that any difference of opinion warrants personal attack. Anger and partisanship arise when individuals assume that a question about their remarks constitutes an attack on themselves as persons. In general, proceeding quietly and calmly will help avoid the appearance of personal attack, but if a member does appear threatened, steps should be taken immediately to reduce his tension.

6. Each member ought to regard himself as having potential value to the discussion leader. His problems should be understood and his attempts to resolve conflict, to summarize, and to bring about balanced contribution should be assisted by all members. The more each member becomes problem-centered and thinks empathetically about the problems of leadership, the more likely it is that discussion will stay on the track.

7. In group discussion, each member should, insofar as possible, consider himself a **group member** rather than an autonomous individual. Introspective remarks are disconcerting to others. Communication in discussion must be mutual. It is not communication **to** other people, but communication **with** them. The goal is understanding. Each member should contribute all he can to the achievement of that goal.

FOUR

Problem—solving discussion

What is problem solving?

Problem solving is a process carried on by an individual or group to find release from tension. Any frustration of goal-seeking behavior presents an obstacle which leads to tension. Achieving this goal by overcoming obstacles and relieving tension is the goal of problem solving.

Problems of survival and reproduction are basic to human existence. More sophisticated are problems of mastery of the environment and satisfaction of personality needs. Our complex society poses few simple and direct problems. Primitive man would face a problem when there was no food in the bin, or when a predator approached. The methods of solving the problem would be obvious—get food or kill the beast. Man, however, is essentially weak. Very early in his existence he found it necessary to band together with others to contend with his problems. While this made it easier to gather food and defend against enemies, coming together in groups generated new problems—those of identity, role, personality projection, status, and obtaining physical comfort and ease—which were more subtle than those of simple survival.

The group helped solve basic human problems but presented new ones, concomitants of group living. The easy resolution of group problems was to select the strongest man in the group as leader. He decided on solutions and the rest of the group carried them out.

Dissatisfaction with this type of leadership arose when it became obvious that the authoritarian took his own needs into account first. The desire to diffuse the benefits of society partially influenced the development of more democratic methods of problem solving. The growing complexity of an industrial society reinforced this trend. Today, though authoritarian control exists on many levels, the group-achieved solution is more and more widely sought.

Problem-solving groups can work on any or all of three levels. The levels are "nested," that is, the most complex includes the two simpler levels. In order of increasing complexity, they are the levels of fact, value, and policy. Some groups may be interested only in determining what the "facts are" about a problem. The information gathered may then be referred to a group whose job it is to evaluate the problem and determine how serious it is. A subsequent group can then work out the actual solution. Most groups, however, are required to grapple with their problem on all three levels. A complete job of problem solving begins with an investigation to obtain a clear picture of the problem. Next, the group must assess the gravity of the problem and the requirements of a solution. Finally, a solution must be developed and set into operation.

The three levels of problem solving are not essential to educational and therapeutic discussion. However, a classroom discussion may pass through analogous stages. The individual receiving therapy will embody the three levels in his personal problem solving. The difference lies more in formalization of procedure than in necessary content. In problem-solving discussion, it is necessary to preserve some rigidity in agenda, so that the group passes consciously through the various steps. In discussion that is not primarily directed to problem solving it is not so necessary to mark this progression, though it will undoubtedly occur if the group is doing a satisfactory job.

The role of the standard agenda

The goal of problem solving is "output" in the form of a solution to a problem. Sometimes the output is a written report which lays down broad lines of policy. Sometimes it is a program put into operation. Each policy-making or problem-solving group must determine its own needs, but it must be clear on what is expected of it.

Once the decision has been made about the form of discussion output, the standard agenda for problem solving can be followed as rigidly as the group feels necessary.

The chart in Figure 1 details the steps of the standard agenda. As

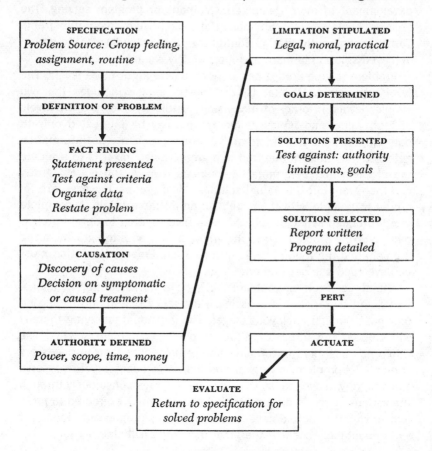

Figure 1. Steps in the Standard Agenda for Problem-Solving

each step is discussed it will be useful to refer back to the chart and note its location in relation to the other steps.

The standard agenda: specification and definition

Before a group can get on with problem solving, members must agree

about the limits of their problem. Perfect agreement would be desirable but impossible. In preliminary discussions, sufficient facts
may not be available to enable the group to see the problem clearly.
It is imperative, however, to agree about the facts needed, if the
group is to confine itself to discussion of the appropriate problem.
If the problem has been referred by an outside source, clarification
can be achieved by checking directly with the person or agency that
referred the problem. If the problem has been developed by the group,
then agreement must be reached on the meaning of the words and
ideas in the problem. There are four major questions a group must
answer in defining a problem.

Does the problem fall within the legitimate purview of the group?
Occasionally groups attempt to solve problems that are none of their
concern. This is impractical and time-wasting and may lead to conflict with groups whose business it is to work on the problem. Well-
meaning citizens groups often vex regular problem-solving agencies
by setting up groups without power or authority to attempt to solve
problems that are already under consideration by legitimate bodies.

In academic discussion, groups may deal with any problem they
like. A problem-solving group, however, must have some stake in the
solution and some standing in the organization or community which
the problem affects. If it does not, it is not necessarily barred from
discussing the question, but it must recognize that its deliberations
will be more a learning experience than an influential contribution
to solution—unless, of course, it is willing to assume the obligations
of a lobbying or public-persuasion group designed to implement
whatever solution it discovers.

Is the problem pertinent? Groups may feel comfortable engaging
in postmortems, solving problems that are already solved, or anticipating problems that have little chance of arising. It is easier to
work with problems like these than with real ones. A group does not
have to worry about implementing a solution to a problem that has
already been solved or does not really exist. The group must examine
its problem question to see whether or not it has some immediacy
and reality. "Immediacy" means that now, or in the foreseeable
future, the problem can be expected to occur. "Reality" means that
the problem is based on observable phenomena, not visceral "feelings" about a situation. When a problem seems based on a "feeling"

that something is wrong, the group must list the facts or observable events that will enable them to specify the problem, its location, and scope.

Does the problem refer to something about which data can be gathered? In order to achieve a real solution, the group must start with a real problem. Internal feelings cannot be considered except in terms of the behavior they cause. Abstract words in a problem statement must be referred to concrete phenomena. For example, little can be done about "morale" in student dorms, but a great deal can be done about the specific activities that may be called "lack of morale." If students are boycotting school events or protesting about the food service, these ought to be the focus of problem solving. It is impossible to solve an abstraction.

Does the wording of the question allow the widest possible latitude for investigation? Inappropriate wording of the question can dictate an erroneous solution. The question, "How can truculence among students be eliminated?" suggests at the outset that students are at fault for whatever is happening. The group may neglect other possible causes of the problem as they respond to the loaded word "truculence."

Open-ended phrasing confers the widest latitude for exploration. The more leeway in the question, the more margin the group will have in proposing solutions. Phrasing a question to allow only two alternatives begs the question and can lead to a split in the group. Questions like "How can the administration in our college be improved?" are preferable to "Should our president be fired?"

Any group member who does not understand the problem will be an impediment to the group. Care must be taken to avoid irrelevancies that arise when some members do not understand the question. Where there is insufficient understanding of the scope and intent of the question, the group is in danger of misdirection. Where the question is too rigidly phrased, the group's potential is limited. Time spent at definition is not wasted. It will spare the group much unnecessary wrangling later on by keeping all members focused on the same problem, thus reducing ambiguity. The group should, of course, reserve the right to return to definition whenever it becomes apparent that lack of understanding of the question is retarding group progress.

The standard agenda: getting the facts

Every group needs specific information about its problem. It must know what is happening, to whom, where, and hopefully, why. Intelligent fact gathering helps the group specify its question and gives it the best chance to discover pertinent facts.

The purpose of fact finding is to provide the members of the group with a body of common knowledge about their problem which they can use as a basis for discovery of causes to which solutions can be applied.

The process of fact finding consists of pooling the information resources of the members. Each person, if he desires, offers a statement of fact for the group to evaluate. Those who pass the tests for facts become part of the data pool.

Some operational definitions for "fact" useful to discussion groups are:

1. A fact is an occurrence reported by a competent viewer or an existing situation which can be perceived by others.
2. A fact is a set of numerical data that conforms to the rules of statistical method.
3. A fact is a statement about events made by a qualified authority.
4. By exclusion: a fact is not an inference, opinion, attitude, or expression of evaluation.

To distinguish factual statements from other types, some critical tests can be employed. Refer to the sources listed in the bibliography for some basic works on identification and evaluation of facts.

Criteria for examination of facts

A fact is not an evaluation or inference. It is easy to confuse types of statements. An inference is a statement about the past or future based on whatever knowledge about the present is available. Inferential statements can be evaluated according to degrees of probability—something or other is likely to happen or to have happened. A factual statement refers to reality. Whatever is asserted as a fact must be observable by others.

A statement like "John is a good man" sounds as if it is factual. It is not. It is a subjective evaluation. All that can be done is to agree or disagree with it. Factual statements can be constructed out of the phenomena that led to the opinion: "John gave $500 to the charity drive," "John attends church regularly," "John does not smoke or drink," etc. Whether these statements would lead everyone to conclude that John was a "good man" is questionable. Evaluations and inferences should be excluded from lists of factual statements.

Facts must be current. College students, especially, have the habit of visiting the library and using the first book they find on a topic. Rarely do they look at the publication date. But conditions constantly change. What may have been "true" in 1950 is not necessarily so today. Out-of-date information is pertinent only to a historical investigation. The criterion of currency may occasionally prevent discovery of good ideas in older sources. However, most vital material is cited again in more current publications. There is only a limited amount of material that a fact-finding group can screen efficiently, and if it shows some care about currency it will find what it needs in more modern sources without multiplying the complexity of its problem by searching older literature.

Facts must be drawn from acceptable authorities. There are few areas of discussion potentially so fraught with emotion as that of the qualification of authorities. Most of us have our heroes—usually they are the famous men who happen to agree with us. But fact finding is not a persuasive process. The group should not be seeking documentation for preconceived ideas, but information from authorities qualified to present it.

An authority is a professional in his field. He has knowledge and understands his own inadequacies. He bases his opinions on current and substantial information. He applies his authority only to his own field.

No authority can be totally bias-free. He is entitled to express opinions which the group may accept to the extent that they accept his qualifications. His opinions should be clearly labeled as such. Any authority whose position confers a bias that would cause him to distort facts should be regarded as suspect, and any authority that does not have technical competence in the area in which he purports to be an authority should be rejected entirely.

Statistical statements must be tested. It is often convenient to present factual material in statistical form. Statistics help the group understand trends as well as the present situation. Because statistics are expressions of norms, there may be exceptional circumstances in the problem under consideration that are not described by the numbers. If all the problems of a similar type were exactly alike, then one solution would suffice for all of them. Statistical information helps to reveal the extent to which situations are alike, but it does not explicate the differences. These must be sought by the group.

Statistical statements may also express causal relationships. It is wise to have someone available who can interpret widely used statistics like "t," "F," and "chi square." Statistics based on the mathematics of probability are being used more and more frequently to report data. The layman cannot be expected to have technical knowledge about their meaning. When information of this sort is discovered, an expert should be called on for help if there is no one in the group capable of interpreting it.

Statements from eyewitnesses must be confirmed. Every individual has personal experiences that are meaningful to him alone. Each man's observation of events is necessarily colored by the way in which he experiences the world. It is virtually impossible for individuals to relate from memory accurate reports of events that happened to them in the past. It is unwise to rely on eyewitness reports unless the salient features of the report are confirmed by other witnesses. Generally, only when several independent reports indicate that an event actually happened can evidence of this sort be relied on. There is an old proverb, "For example is no proof." Fact-finding groups should take particular care to determine that facts accepted are real and representative rather than imaginary or exceptional.

Statements of fact must be related to the problem. Some problem-solving groups apparently operate on the principle that, if they cannot find facts pertinent to the question, they will develop a question pertinent to the facts they can find. This is not suggested operating procedure for groups whose future might be affected by their success or failure at solving the problem they were expected to solve.

Many problems are very poorly phrased, and it is only after fact finding that the question can be reworded to make real sense. When facts seem to alter the intent of the question, it is wise to check back with the referral source to determine whether the new question correctly expresses what he had in mind. Confining examination only to available facts may be digressive and prevent a thorough search for pertinent information.

The group may have to seek information from outside sources. It should not be assumed that there is sufficient information present in the group to justify omission of outside research. Libraries and outside experts should be used as widely as they are necessary and available.

Group research

Most problems are so complex that it would be wasteful if each member attempted an independent investigation. The group can be divided into subgroups charged with investigating a phase of the problem and reporting back to the group. The group must first ask, "What must we know in order to deal with this problem adequately?" and "Where can we find the information?" Some groups recommend that members prepare an outline of their individual research. Such preparation may be useful in an academic context to help motivate participation, but in problem solving it must be recognized that it may also produce advocates. More important, it does not guarantee that relevant information will be uncovered. One member may be captivated by an obscure phase of the problem and overwhelm the group with information about his special interest. The picture of the problem may be distorted by the one-sided presentation. In addition to aiding the integration of personalities with the group goal, joint research is a more thorough way of obtaining necessary information than individual effort.

Redefining the problem

Ample time should be allowed for fact finding, for no matter how thoroughly the group searches, they will never find all they need. The group should not be so critical, however, that they demand that all the facts be discovered. There is no human problem on which anyone can obtain all the facts. When the members are satisfied that their major questions have been relatively well answered, they can move on to the next step with the understanding that at any time in the discussion it becomes evident that further material is necessary, they may return to fact finding.

When the group is satisfied that it has sufficient information, the problem should be re-examined in the light of the facts. If the question has been poorly worded, sufficient clarification can be made to enable the group to proceed to the discovery of causes more efficiently.

Rewording follows much the same procedure as the initial definition of the problem. Once again, the group must determine whether the problem is pertinent and worth solving. It must check, once more, whether the problem still falls within their scope of authority or whether it expresses the needs of the referral agency. Finally, this is the last chance to be sure that the problem is appropriately worded. There can be no tolerance for ambiguity, for this final rewording will lay out the dimensions of subsequent deliberations. The end result of problem-solving discussion is a solution designed to eliminate a particular problem. The question should be sufficiently specific that solutions can be explicit rather than vague recommendations incapable of implementation. It should be clear enough to serve as a check for solutions—"Will the proposal really solve this problem?"

An evaluative assessment may be inserted in this phase of discussion also. Once the facts have been gathered, the group can determine whether the problem is serious enough to warrant a solution now. It can compare the problem with other problems to determine which should be dealt with first. The group has the option of separating out parts of their problem for immediate solution and leaving other aspects for later deliberations or other groups.

Fact finding is hard work. It is easy to get impatient and be superficial, but the group must persist until it has completed the job. The temptation to "catch fire" at some startling bit of information and jump quickly to a dramatic solution must be resisted. Fact finding tests the willingness of group members to confront their problem realistically. This step of the agenda is vital because it is the foundation for everything else that is to happen in the discussion.

The standard agenda: discovery of causes

A "cause" is a statement that purports to explain why something happens. Solutions to problems may be directed to the symptoms of the problem, to causes of the symptoms, or to both. A good physician may prescribe palliatives for fever and headache in order to ease symptoms. But he will not stop there. He will examine his patient carefully to find the causes of symptoms so that he can treat them also. The analogy to problem-solving groups is appropriate.

Once facts have been obtained, the problem-solving group must isolate causes of the conditions it has found. A variety of symptoms can be traced back to a single cause. Symptomatic treatment would not eliminate the problem but would merely ease it temporarily. What the group seeks is a statement about the reasons for the trouble against which they can direct solutions. It is easy for the group to go astray at this point. The most obvious way to state causes is in terms of attitudes and feelings. A statement like ". . . the reason is that students just don't have the right attitude" both overstates and is insufficiently specific. It is an expression of an evaluation that cannot be measured or verified.

Nebulous statements of cause direct the group to unworkable solutions. In the early days of the civil-rights movement sincere people concluded that faulty Negro-white relations were caused by "lack of mutual respect." A number of absurd solutions arose from this analysis. Whites would invite Negroes to their homes and embarrass them with patronizing oversolicitousness. Negroes would make whites feel "at ease" by telling jokes on themselves. Students would locate the one Negro enrolled in their school and elect him to some minor office, qualified or not. Real progress did not take place until it was realized that solutions directed against attitudes could not work. Effectual solutions had to be directed against the reasons for the defective attitudes, reasons found in the social, political, and economic problems that lay at the heart of the difficulty. The problem of attitudes was part, not all, of the question. Attitudes resulted in barring Negroes from the ballot box and denying them adequate housing or jobs, which in turn led to demands for solution. The facts in the case were the various racial incidents, riots, and demonstrations. Immediate causes were political inequities, squalor, and social disqualification. Sermons about attitudes of individuals were futile until organized pressure was exerted to eliminate ghettolike slums, enlarge the franchise, and provide work. Even then, it is obvious that a long time must elapse before constructive change in attitudes will come about.

Attitudes are cloudy, personal, difficult to understand and change. Law is tangible, obvious, and capable, at least, of partial administration. Faulty attitudes have resulted in defective law, or perhaps the reverse was the case. Solutions, however, have to be directed against tangibles. If a group decides that attitude change is necessary, it had best be prepared for a long-range solution, accompanied every step of the way by intermediate programs directed at observable, manageable causes.

Given a choice between something measurable and something unmeasurable, it is generally wiser to attempt to deal with the former. If a doctor says that the patient will "pull through" if he can get enough plasma and "develop a will to live," the most obvious step is to insert a plasma tube immediately and then worry about the "will to live." It is entirely possible that the introduction of fresh blood might change the patient's attitude anyway, exactly as it is possible that fresh legislation or a new program might alter beliefs.

Suggested causes should be evaluated to determine whether something can be done about them. The group should not jump immediately to a discussion of solutions. They must be sure that solutions are possible, however. If causes cannot be delineated with precision, it may be necessary for the group to deal with symptoms, at least until further investigation brings causes to light that can be dealt with.

Such a prosaic approach to causation seems to leave no room for idealistic, creative solutions. However, if there is a workable idea latent in a statement of cause, the group should be able to spot where the statement can be translated into action. If a statement of cause cannot be made real, it may mean that the group is not adequately creative or imaginative. Sometimes, what appears to be idealistic and imaginative is actually an evasion of problem-solving responsibility. The member who calls for a "bold program to strike at the roots of the problem in the hearts and minds of men" is not being idealistic so much as self-righteous. Self-righteousness is a method of seeking social approval by avoiding the realities of action while making a pretense of action. The self-righteous cause ("if everyone were only exactly like good, old me!") is impossible to eliminate.

Sometimes in educational discussion, students attempt to do what the greatest minds of the century would not dare tackle. They state the cause of all the problems in American foreign policy in a single statement ("the cause is unawareness on our part of the strivings of the former colonial peoples") and conclude with a solution statement that reads like a sermon ("we must all bend our efforts to greater understanding of the suppressed masses of the world"). Such groups pride themselves on their creativity, but they have created nothing but a mass of words. Unless the words can be transformed into action that can be taken by someone, they are worthless. If there is nothing in a reported solution that can be enacted or programmed by some responsible agency or executive, then the group has not done an adequate job. Even if the group has no authority and can do nothing itself, its recommendations should detail a job that can be done by someone. Only if causes have been specified with precision can a group arrive at a sensible conclusion.

The standard agenda: assessing authorities and limitations

Before beginning to propose solutions, the problem-solving group must take a hard-headed appraisal of the scope of its authority. Such an understanding will shape their solutions. It makes a real difference in proposing solutions whether a group can take action or must recommend a solution to someone else. An action group must present an operations plan with its solution. A recommending group need not, but it should be prepared to defend the operational capability of its proposal.

Authority. Few problem-solving groups have the authority to administer their solution. Most have only the power to recommend. Their proposals must be approved by someone else—an executive, or the membership of a large group.

Where solutions must be approved elsewhere, the group should determine boundaries for their recommended solutions. Solutions previously adopted may provide guidelines for them. If the problem seems to require a drastically different approach, the group may have to prepare a defense for their solution. The group must remember that the approving authority has not had the benefit of orderly process through the steps of problem solving and might not understand why the solution selected is necessary.

Group goals are limited by the nature of the source of approval. This does not mean that the group should seek acceptance for an inadequate solution. It must understand, however, that it may have to prove the worth of its proposal. Some deference to the approving authority is imperative to preserve some of the proposed program. It is demoralizing to have a perfectly good proposal rejected because it exceeded some executive's tolerance limits. The group must maintain a realistic attitude and recognize that partial success is generally preferable to total failure.

When the group is to administer its own solution, it must be aware of its own executive capabilities and its relationship to other problem-solving and administrative divisions in the larger organization. When referral of the program is to be made, the group must also consider the nature and capacity of those who will be responsible for carrying it out.

Limitations. Solutions that are excessively expensive, take too long, demand unavailable resources, or have unrealistic requirements for personnel are likely to be rejected when submitted for approval. A distinction must be made between what is possible and what it would be "nice" to be able to do.

It is easy for planners to dispose of other people's money. It is not difficult to specify a sum of money needed for a proposal; it is harder to construct a solution to fit the money available. Many groups with apparently good solutions meet failure when an administrator tries to act on their recommendations and discovers that he does not have sufficient resources to permit him to approve it. The group that wants its solution to work must consider limitations of time, personnel, and money before it begins to consider solutions. Proposals should include a budget detailing sources of funds as well as a list of personnel needed, material required, suggested administrative structure, and proposed length of operation.

Solutions must also take cognizance of existing activities. New undertakings cannot be allowed to drain resources from necessary, ongoing programs. Newly initiated enterprises must fit the existing structure of activity. If they interfere unduly with what is currently going on, new problems, potentially more severe, may result.

Idealism sometimes impels groups to call for "crash programs" to solve their problem. They feel that anything that gets in the way of their solution ought to be crushed. However, "crash programs" are only needed to solve "crash problems." If a group finds itself getting overwrought about the urgent need for its solution, it may need to return to its definition of the problem to re-evaluate whether such urgency is warranted. The members may have had their judgmental vision distorted by immersion in their problem and have not adequately measured its relative severity compared with other problems.

Groups are also limited in their activities by legal and moral considerations. No one expects the members of a planning group to be trained attorneys. Certain manifest legalities must be observed, however. It is not wise to assert, as so many groups do, that "laws can be changed" to accommodate their ideas. The smug answer may have no relation to reality if they cannot also present a proposal to bring about the necessary legislative enactments.

Virtually all companies and government agencies have legal departments to check on implications of proposed programs. Groups that do not receive regular legal advice should consider obtaining it. A citizen's group dealing with control of "indecent literature," for example, may run afoul of the law even before solutions are proposed. Their very conversation may be slanderous in context. Legal advice sought early is insurance against failure.

Moral limitations must also be imposed. A group may want to remedy a problem but not badly enough to interfere with something else. In trying to control delinquency in a school district, for example, the group might want to specify that the solution should not impose excessive burdens on teachers or resort to undemocratic methods.

It is usually assumed that if a goal is approved, the intermediate steps to that goal are also approved. This implies that the end justifies the means. Citizens of a democracy will not want to use undemocratic procedures, even to achieve a thoroughly democratic objective. A moral end, logically, could not be achieved by immoral means. For this reason, problem-solving groups will want to take some time to examine their values and motives in order to impose moral restrictions on themselves. Those rights that the group pledges itself to respect ought to be listed. At times, under pressure of problem solving, a group may be tempted to indulge in immoralities for purposes of expediency. Conscious awareness of moral obligations will tend to prevent this.

The standard agenda: developing solutions

A solution can be phrased as a description of activities, reported as a list of steps in a program, or presented as a statement of policy sufficiently specific that an administrator can be guided by it. Precision in developing solutions is materially assisted by the preparation of a list of "goal" statements that serve as check points for the group to determine when they have achieved their solution requirements.

Goals are inherent in the problem question and are molded by the authority and limitations of the group. They are used as standards against which to evaluate proposals. Those proposals or parts of proposals that satisfy one or more goal statements without violating the authority and limitations are acceptable. For example, a list of goals for the solution to the academic problem dealing with required and elective courses for students might read:

1. The solution must increase the number of electives permitted the student.
2. The solution must not add new courses to the catalogue.
3. The solution must not interfere with academic freedom.
4. The solution must require no additional personnel.
5. The solution must maintain requirements sufficient to co-ordinate with other universities.
6. The solution must not involve coercion of students.

Statements about desired ends are intermingled with those about authorities and limitations. In preparing a solution, the group can refer to the list to ensure that the eventual program or policy meets the requirements set by the group for itself.

Once developed, the list of goals should be examined to see how many are presently being met by existing programs. The group should strive to achieve only those goals which are not satisfied by existing programs.

If the facts are clear and the goals simple, a solution might read: "A training program should be set up for dorm counselors administered by the office of the dean of men." Training content can be specified: "Counselors should learn to isolate problems in their dorms and be familiar with referral procedures." An additional statement about time and place and projected budget should be added.

Most problems cannot be solved this simply. More often, groups face problems for which various alternatives are available. Each must be checked against the goals, and only those which meet the requirements approved. The statements accepted as a solution should be checked for redundancy and appraised once more for the way in which they are adjusted to authorities and limitations of the group. It may be helpful to have members role-play administrators to raise questions about details of the solution. The group has the option to accept a symptomatic, causal, or combination solution. The approach will be determined by the list of goals.

While development of solutions is a collective activity, consensus on wording of a solution is not sufficient to warrant putting it out as a report. Consensus must also take place on whether the solution is workable. A solution should be evaluated against five basic principles.

1. It must (if not a symptomatic solution) be directed at pertinent causes.
2. It must be relevant to the factual context of the problem.
3. It must not exceed the authority of the group.
4. It must be within the limitations of the group.
5. It must improve present conditions by eliminating or alleviating some part or all of the problem.

If the solution is to be phrased as a program, particular care must be exercised to avoid nebulous and ambiguous wording. Program planners must recognize that the words in their solutions must be transformed into action which will be allowed to proceed for a time and then tested to determine effectiveness; it is only at that point that the planners can assess their own ability as problem solvers. The fact of consensus is not the same as the fact of successful operation. For groups of this sort, an operations procedure is necessary.

The pragmatic approach necessary for problem-solving groups in business, government, or the community differs from the requirements of educational or therapeutic discussion. Problem solving may have both educational and therapeutic concomitants. The group may feel that they learned something and experience relief and euphoria at completion. These feelings are desirable, but they are not the main goal of problem solving. Members of such groups can be thoroughly disgruntled with their solution, and yet the solution can be deemed a good one because it works.

The standard agenda: program planning with PERT

The quasi-mathematical procedure called PERT (Program Evaluation and Review Technique) provides the problem-solving group with a method for developing a workable operations plan. PERT can be applied to any program proposal that consumes time. PERT measures whether a program will be completed on schedule, as well as enabling a planning group to review its program in diagram form to detect its errors. PERT does not make automatic decisions for an administrator. It reveals to him the kinds of decisions he might be called on to make and shows him what they might have to be made about. PERT was developed by the United States Navy in 1958 to solve some of the problems of coordinating the Polaris guided-missile program. Because it can easily be accommodated to general program planning, it was adopted by many businesses and government bureaus. Today, most government contractors are required to use PERT, for it has been discovered that it can be used to co-ordinate apparently unrelated activities.

A planning group using PERT is able to detect impending bottlenecks, allocate personnel appropriately, estimate reasonable deadlines, determine starting times, and investigate the logic of the program. Complex operations must be handled by a computer; for most groups, however, the arithmetic of PERT is simple enough to be done with paper and pencil.[1]

Case study of a problem-solving discussion employing PERT.[2]

The case presented here will demonstrate how PERT affects problem solving. This case will be referred to as a model as each step of the PERT process is discussed.

Early in 1964, a group of public health officials received complaints about "smog" from the citizens of Green City. They were assigned by the state public-health director to propose a program to solve the problem.

Phase 1. The group defined the question. "Smog" was defined as "polluted air." This definition had a technical meaning; air was considered polluted when it contained a specific proportion of impurities. They phrased the problem, "What can be done by any state or

[1]Early in 1964, the Western Branch of the American Public Health Association began a series of seminars designed to teach PERT to administrators and planners associated with community health agencies. The seminars included training in the standard discussion agenda as well as specific direction in the steps of PERT programming. Students at the seminars gave glowing testimonials about the effect of PERT on planning in their agencies. The seminars are continuing and Western Branch is preparing a book about the use of PERT in small-agency planning. Information can be obtained by writing Dr. Mary Arnold, School of Public Health, University of California, Berkeley, Calif., or James L. Bemis, Department of Speech, Olympic College, Bremerton, Wash.
[2]The case detailed here is one the writer became familiar with in his capacity as PERT consultant.

local agency or this group to reduce or eliminate the polluted air in Green City?"

Phase 2. Facts were presented. Items pertaining to temporary pollution by forest fires were rejected. Facts were admitted about (1) emission of smoke and noxious gases by a paper-pulp mill in the area, (2) the land configuration in the valley where Green City is located, and (3) prevailing winds and weather conditions. It was conceded that nothing could be done about the weather or land configurations, but that both contributed to the pollution problem. Data on car exhausts as sources of pollution were rejected as not sufficiently severe. The community record of the pulp mill was deemed admissable. The mill had refused compliance with a voluntary pollution-abatement program last year. Data were also admitted about community attitudes toward the mill. The general feeling among residents seemed to be that the mill would close down rather than comply with abatement restrictions.

Phase 3. The problem was restated: "What can be done by local authorities to obtain compliance with minimum standards of air-pollution control by the XXX Pulp Mill?" "Minimum standards" was understood by the group as equipment—estimated cost, $127,000—that would result in abatement.

Phase 4. Causes were sought in the past behavior of the mill in relation to pollution: (1) the millowners had expressed the attitude that, as the mill was the main industry of the area, they were apparently immune to pressures for compliance; (2) the mill was heavily mortgaged and the expenditure of $127,000 for installation of equipment would result in serious financial difficulty; and (3) the community felt that nothing could be done about the mill anyway.

The group agreed that the hostile public attitude of the millowners may have been the result of their financial situation. The real questions appeared to be how the mill could be helped to finance installation of equipment, and how community pressure could be used to prod the millowners to take action.

Phase 5. The group defined its power as "recommending and public relations." Some Green City officials were members, so that there was access to appropriate authorities. Time available was stipulated as "as soon as possible." Money was "budget allotted by state." Personnel was "those present and anyone else induced to participate." The group agreed that anything mandatory they proposed would have to be enacted by the Green City Council. Moral limitations were that nothing could be done that would force the mill out of the valley. Practical limitations were funds available from any source to pay for installation of equipment.

Phase 6. The group stated its goals:

1. Any solution must materially abate pollution from the XXX Mill.
2. Voluntary compliance would be preferred.
3. Legislation is necessary to ensure no future malfeasance.
4. Community support must be mobilized behind any program.
5. Program for community support would involve use of mass media.

Phase 7. The solution was:

1. Submit to the council an ordinance requiring all industry in Green City to install abatement devices if they contributed more than 1 per cent of the total pollution. Companies so required were to be exempted from 50 per cent of real property taxes until 75 per cent of the value of the equipment had been recovered.
2. Public-information program to precede presentation of legislative proposal. Use of local television station for program on dangers of pollution.
3. Various other solutions were adopted. We will concern ourselves with the development of the television program.

It was at this point that the group began to use PERT. Refer to Figure 2 (page 92) as each step of PERT is discussed.

PERT I. Stipulate final event or occurrence marking completion of program.

The word "event" is the key to PERT. It means "an occurrence that takes no time, but marks the start or end of a process or activity." For example, "closing the door" is not an event. It is a statement of activity. The event would be "door closed," which describes the state at the end of the process of door closing. "Knob touched" might be the event that denotes the beginning of the process. Everything between "knob touched" and "door closed" would be part of the process of "entering the room."

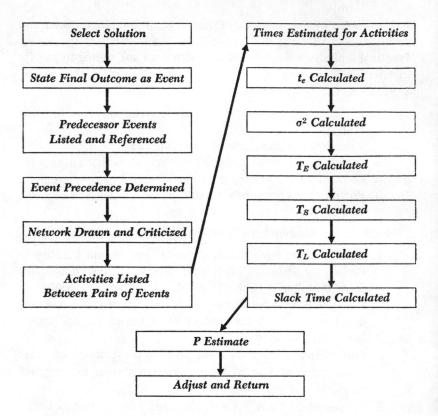

Figure 2. The PERT Process

The first step taken by the Green City group was to identify the event that marked the end of their job, the presentation of a television program. The final event was named "television program signed off."

It is difficult to think in terms of events. Most people think in processes so complex that "planning a television program" would sound simple to them. Planning such a program, however, is complex and consists of many other activities, thus calling for allocation of resources. Each activity, up to the final event, has some other activity dependent on it. Events are points (in space) that mark where activities start and end. They are reference points on a PERT diagram.

Events should be regarded as locations on the map of the program. The lines that connect events represent activities that must be carried on between them. The complex of events (locations) and activities (connecting lines) constitute a model of the program solution.

PERT II. List events that must happen before the final event can happen.

After the final event has been specified, the planning group brainstorms on the topic: "What must happen before this end point can be reached?" Note: "What must happen?" not "What must we do?" The group focuses on events, not activities.

Events need not be listed in chronological order. If the members have omitted any major events they will be able to insert them when they draw their network. Some events may refer to trivial activities. This will not disturb the plan. As long as an event is logically precedent to the final event, it will fit neatly into the diagram. Only illogical or unnecessary events will disturb the diagram.

The Air-pollution Group listed the events precedent to the end of the television program. They had decided on a thirty-minute documentary film to be followed by a panel discussion of the implications of the film. See Figure 3 (page 94) for their lists of events. The events were not listed in chronological order. When the diagram is drawn, they will fall into logical order. The next step is to give reference designations to each event.

It is irrelevant what the references are. They can be numbers, "1, 2, 3, etc.," or letters, "A, B, C, etc.," or names, "Plan, Door, Fix, etc.," so long as it is possible to reference from list to diagram. Numbers are recommended because they are easier to work with in the computer. References do not specify the order of occurrence of events, only locations on the diagram.

The Green City group discovered two events on their list that appeared to be unnecessary: "other districts informed" and "phone calls made to discussants." They deleted these because they decided that notification was provided for in their regular routine and the item about phone calls did not fit the criteria for events. Later on, we will discuss what the consequences would have been had they left them in.

A PERT group is not bound by its original event list. Any event may be dropped; any event may be added. Neither is there reason to be concerned about maintaining the integrity of numerical sequence. The numbers refer only to location, not order.

PERT III. Determine necessary, immediate, precedent events.

If an event list is very long it is useful to attempt to sort events into a rough time order to facilitate determination of necessary precedence. With a short list like the one in Figure 3 (below), it is not necessary. At best, however, only a rough approximation of order is possible, since most programs include simultaneous events.

Necessity is the sole criterion for determining precedence. Attention must be on **what has to happen** before each event. With event 4, "film taken from mailbox," it can be shown that **immediately** preceding it must be some statement about ordering the film. Event 2, "film order placed in mail," seems to do this. No other event on the list

Figure 3. PERT events and reference designations

Reference	Event	Precedent
1	Planning-committee meeting adjourned	0*
2	Film order dropped in mail	3
3	Final vote on selection of film taken	5
4	Film taken from mailbox	2
	Other districts informed	
5	Approval letter from supervisor received	6
6	Campaign proposal presented to supervisor	1
7	Meeting with station manager adjourned	3
8	Publicity mailed to newspaper	17
9	Schedule confirmation received	7
10	Last spot announcement ends	11
	Phone calls made to discussants	
11	Spot-announcement drafts completed	3, 15
12	Film presented to production manager	4
13	Film discussants seated in studio	15
14	Film discussants selected	3
15	Invitations to discussants dropped in mail	14
16	Acceptance letter from last discussant received	15
17	Publicity drafts approved	9, 16
18	Final event: Television program signed off	10, 12, 13, 8

*Present meeting referenced as event 0.

can immediately precede 4, so 2 is named as the **immediate, precedent** event, coming **necessarily** before 4.

"Immediately" means that no other event on the list intervenes. Several things can happen immediately before an event. If they do not interfere with each other, they are all designated as necessary, precedent events. The table in Figure 3 shows how the Green City list looked after necessary precedents had been found for each event.

"Necessity" is essential in determining precedents. Once the group exercised its free choice to determine what it wanted to do, logic determines procedure.

PERT IV. Develop a diagram showing connection of events.

The next step in PERT is to draw a diagram connecting the events. Figure 4 (page 96) diagrams the television program. Events are connected in their necessary relationship. The lines between events indicate activities that must be carried on between events. The length of activity lines does not indicate time between events. They express relationship only.

The blank PERT diagram is useful in many ways. If the group had left "informing other districts" on their list as event 19, it would have been preceded necessarily by 16, "acceptance of discussants," but it did not necessarily precede any other event. That portion of the diagram would have looked like this:

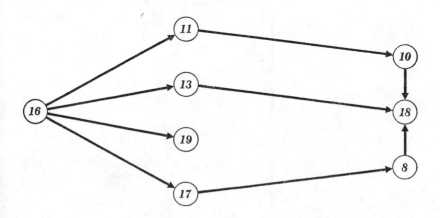

Event 19 would be "dangling" and thus disclosed as irrelevant. Ac-

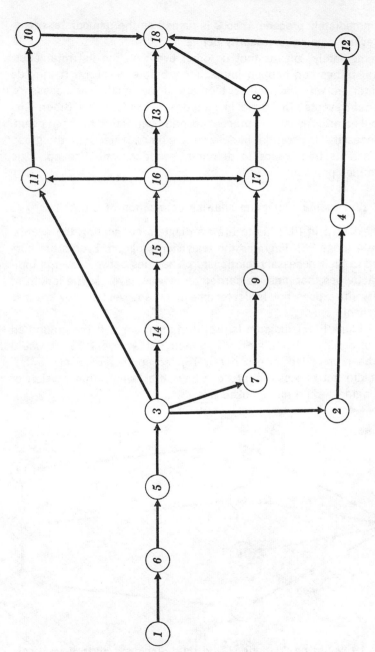

Figure 4. PERT Diagram of television program displaying dependency of events

tivities between 16 and 19 would be unnecessary. Where a dangling event appears in a PERT diagram, the group must decide whether it is essential to the accomplishment of the goal or should be dropped from the list.

Suppose that in the list of events an item indicating approval from a supervisor was necessary after the discussants and the film had been selected. The diagram would look like this:

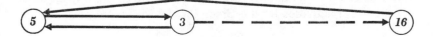

Such a situation is called a "loop." It may mean either that an activity must be carried on through the duration of the program (in this case that the supervisor remain constantly available to give approvals) or that an unnecessary activity is continuing. If supervisory approval is necessary every step of the way, it should be handled through a regular reporting procedure, or built into the activity list. The loop must be removed, either by eliminating a redundant activity or building a rational procedure to handle a repeated activity. PERT shows only that a decision has to be made. The group must make the decision.

The blank PERT diagram is a visual check on the logic of a program plan. The group can detect potential bottlenecks such as event 3, which has four other events dependent on it. Unless and until event 3 is accomplished, work must be delayed on four other tracks. Event 18 illustrates another kind of dependency. Four activities have to be completed before 18 can happen. In either case, a responsible administrator would immediately be able to locate potential difficulties and would have some information about how to deploy resources and personnel to meet them.

PERT V. Enumerate activities to take place between events.

To calculate the probability of successful operation, a careful listing of activities is necessary. An "activity" is whatever must happen between event-reference points.

Companies with regular PERT sections maintain detailed records on job operations. Other groups must rely on the experience of their members, who must list activities on each track. No really important activity may be omitted, though minor details need not be enumerated.

When activities between a pair of events are exceedingly complex, a subgroup may be designated to prepare another diagram for insertion into the master diagram. These are referred to as "sub-PERTs." In industry, higher management works with master diagrams only. Each lower level has its own visual plan. The components are fitted into a master plan for analysis purposes. Refer to Figure 5 (page 100) for the list of activities for the Green City television program.

PERT VI. Estimating times.

A series of estimates is made, based on the activity list. (See Figure 5 for detail on the activity list, with complete computations.) An expected time (t_e) is to be calculated for the activities between each pair of events. To derive t_e, three time estimates are made for each activity. The pessimistic estimate (b) refers to the time an activity would take if everything that could go wrong did go wrong. The optimistic estimate (a) is the fastest time in which a task could be accomplished, if everything went as smoothly as possible. Finally, the time a job is most likely to take (m) is estimated from previous experience or the best educated guess. The expected time (t_e) for each activity is computed from

$$t_e = \frac{a + 4m + b}{6}.$$

t_e is an arithmetic mean based on the assumption that the best and worst have a relatively equal chance of occurrence, whereas the best guess has twice the chance of occurrence as the combination of the other two. It estimates the amount of time an activity is likely to consume. While the estimate may not be exact in any given case, over an entire diagram errors average out, so that this procedure of estimating time has been shown to be statistically reliable.

To determine the influence of possible variations in time estimates on the whole plan, a variance (σ^2) is calculated for each t_e. Variance is based on the amount of influence exerted by the optimistic and pessimistic times on the best guess. The formula for variance is

$$\sigma^2 = \frac{(b - a)^2}{6}.$$

The variance calculation is the basis of the later estimate of the probability of successful completion.

PERT VII. Compare expected completion time and necessary completion time.

The calculation of t_e, or estimated time for an activity, makes it possible to calculate an expected completion time for each event. By comparing expected completion times with the completion date set for the program, the chances of satisfactory operation can be calculated. If no deadline is set, expected completion times can be used to determine when a project is likely to be done.

Figure 6 (page 102) shows the PERT network for the television program with all necessary calculations. Events are designated by reference numbers in circles. Lines and arrows show precedence. Above each event is the calculation of expected completion time (T_E). Below each event is the latest time by which it can be completed (T_L). On the track connecting events is the estimated time (t_e). Below the diagram, z is calculated for determination of probability.

Expected completion time (T_E) is calculated by summing the t_e scores for events along each track. t_e between 1 and 6 = 15.2, so that we can expect 15.2 days to accomplish 6. Since 5 is dependent on 6, we add t_e scores between 6 and 5 to determine T_E for 5. The sum is 25.4. We can expect to achieve 5, "selection of the film," in just about a month, or 25.4 workdays from the start of the project. Of course, much of this is waiting time, and other activities on other projects can take place during this period.

Simple summing of t_e to derive T_E works only when there is one arrow pointing to an event. When there is more than one arrow, T_E is based on the **longest expected completion time.** For example, 17 has two tracks coming in to it. Calculating T_E via 1, 6, 5, 3, 14, 15, 16, 17 equals 113.0. Calculating via 1, 6, 5, 3, 7, 9, 17 equals 118.4 Since 17 depends on completion of **both** tracks, all activities necessary to 17 cannot happen until both tracks are completed. Therefore, the T_E is based on the longest track.

Calculation of T_E for event 18 (the final event) is based on the longest T_E track through the network $(T_E = 126.6)$. The group discovered that the only available date for the show was 125.0 days from

Figure 5. Activities list and calculations for Green City television program

Between events	Activities	a	m	b	t.	σ^2
1 & 6	Committee appointed to write report Report draft written Report approval obtained Deliver report to supervisor	7	14	28	15.2	12.25
6 & 5	Supervisor reads report Supervisor writes approval letter Approval letter sent back to group	7	10	14	10.2	1.37
5 & 3	Committee appointed and meets Films previewed and discussed Acceptance of film Final discussion and vote	21	42	56	40.8	33.99
3 & 2	Letter written Obtain check Mail order Order received by film company	7	10	14	10.2	1.37
3 & 7	Meetings held with station personnel Arrangements made for spot commercials	7	10	14	10.2	1.37
3 & 11	Discussion of copywriters Copywriters interviewed Copywriter hired Drafts written and approved	21	28	35	28.0	5.29
2 & 4	Film shipped from company Film in transit	21	28	35	28.0	5.29
4 & 12	Film inspected for breaks Film taken to television studio	.25	1	2	1.0	.016
12 & 18	Film played on program	.25	.25	.25	.25	0

Figure 5. Activities list and calculations for Green City television program (continued)

Between events	Activities	a	m	b	t.	σ^2
7 & 9	Schedule prepared and approved	7	14	21	14.0	5.29
9 & 17	Drafts written and approved	21	28	35	28.0	5.29
17 & 8	Releases mimeographed and mailed	1	2	3	2.0	.11
8 & 18	Releases received and run five times	5	6	8	6.2	.25
3 & 14	List of possible discussants made up Selection of discussants and alternates Personnel assigned to contact discussants	14	21	28	21.0	5.29
14 & 15	Letters written and mailed Phone calls made where necessary	1	2	3	2.0	.11
15 ⌊ 16	Details given to discussants Alternates arranged if necessary Final confirmations received	7	14	21	14.0	5.29
16 & 13	Give instructions to discussants Hold film preview for discussants Rehearse discussion Pre-program warm-up	14	21	28	21.0	5.29
13 & 18	Waiting time until start of program Watch film and commercial breaks Hold discussion	.1	.1	.1	.1	0
11 & 10	Deliver announcements Allow one week for run	8	12	15	11.8	1.37
10 & 18	Interval to program	.2	.2	.2	.2	0
16 & 17	Biographies and background obtained on discussants	7	10	12	9.8	.69
16 & 11	Names inserted	.1	.1	.1	.1	0

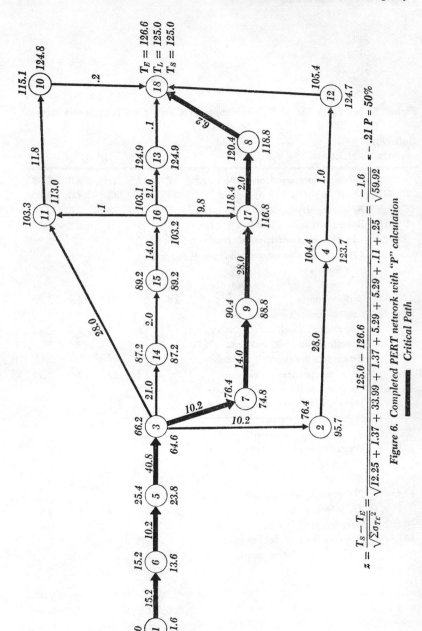

$$z = \frac{T_S - T_E}{\sqrt{\Sigma \sigma_{T_E}^2}} = \frac{125.0 - 126.6}{\sqrt{12.25 + 1.37 + 33.99 + 1.37 + 5.29 + 5.29 + .11 + .25}} = \frac{-1.6}{\sqrt{59.92}} = -.21 \ P = 50\%$$

Figure 6. *Completed PERT network with "P" calculation*
■ *Critical Path*

the start. Because there is no alternative, the latest possible completion date (T_L) must be 125.0 days. This appears impossible to achieve, but the optimistic estimate shows that the group has some chance of success, for it is as likely to occur as the pessimistic estimate. The question is: given the present plan, including commitment of personnel and resources, how good is the chance of getting the program on the air?

To find this out, T_L is calculated for each event by subtracting t_e from T_L cumulatively from the final event back to event 1. The process is the reverse of the T_E calculation: the **smallest** T_L is used for events where two or more paths converge. Slack time is then calculated from $T_L - T_E$ for each event. The track from start to conclusion with the smallest slack time is called "critical path." Slack time may be negative, as it is for the final event, -1.6 (i.e., $126.6 - 125.0$). The group must now make some changes on the critical path if they are to increase their chances of meeting their deadline.

PERT VIII. Calculate probabilities.

Probability estimates are based on the critical path. The administrator who uses the PERT diagram to deploy his personnel will note that the critical path is the greatest potential source of trouble. He may be able to remove persons assigned elsewhere to work on critical-path activities. If he does, it would change time estimates on both paths, and a new critical path must then be calculated based on the new estimates.

The group planning the television program observed that their problem lay in meeting with television personnel and running publicity. Two simple adjustments were made. Extra stenographic help was given the publicity writer and closer phone liaison was developed with the station manager. The two changes materially improved their probability estimate.

The problems on the critical path were easily solved since there was ample personnel available for reassignment. Often, however, it is not so simple. If an administrator is limited in both personnel and resources he has to gamble when he moves resources from one track to another. PERT cannot compensate for the lack of skill and knowledge of an administrator, but it can show planners where to anticipate major decisions and perhaps influence them to scale down the program in cases where the administrator might have to "cut it too close" in order to succeed.

PERT in small-group and agency planning does not require this tight control. A simple probability estimate is sufficient to advise the group that its plan is, or is not, rational. The probability estimate is made by summing the variances for each event along the critical path and calculating z, a statistic associated with a percentage on a normal-probability curve, for the formula

$$z = \frac{T_S - T_E}{\sqrt{\Sigma \sigma_{T_E}^2}}.$$

The calculations for the television program are found in Figure 6.

The question is: how likely is it that the group can make it in 125 days? Calculation showed that they had a 13 per cent chance. (Tables for the association of z with probability can be found in any standard statistics book, as well as in most PERT references.) The chances of completion did not look good. After making the two adjustments, z approximated 0, giving the group a 50 per cent chance. A 50 per cent probability means that just about enough personnel and resources have been committed to do the job. The optimistic and pessimistic estimates have about an equal chance of occuring and cancel each other out. High probability means there is waste somewhere in the program. Low probability means that more effort is needed.

Review of steps in PERT

1. Discussion is completed. Group has defined problem, discovered facts, made statement of causes, determined authority, limitations, and goals, suggested solutions, selected a solution, phrased the solution as a program.

2. Group specifies final event which signals completion of their program.

3. Group lists events that must happen before the final event and assigns reference numbers.

4. Immediate, necessary, precedent events are determined for each event.

5. A PERT diagram is drawn showing connection of events. Extraneous and redundant events are deleted.

6. Activities are listed between each pair of events.

7. Group makes best, worst, most-likely time estimates for activities. t_e calculated for each track. Variances are calculated for each event.

8. Expected completion time is calculated by summation for each event. Where activities converge, maximum T_E is used.

9. Scheduled completion date is determined. Latest allowable time is calculated for each event. Where activities converge, minimum T_L is used.

10. Slack time is calculated for each track to final event. Critical path is drawn based on path with least slack.

11. Probability estimate of satisfactory completion is made based on critical path.

The planning group remains intact throughout. PERT is a group process demanding the pooling of individual talents. No one person is qualified to use PERT alone unless it involves only his own activities.

PERT and the standard agenda

The emphasis of educational discussion is on interpersonal process, primarily, with interest in personal gains in knowledge and understanding considered more important than group achievement. The assumption of both educational and therapeutic discussion is that satisfactory interpersonal process will lead to satisfactory outcomes. Sufficient evidence is available that interaction between people can influence the outcome of discussion groups. Both educational and therapeutic discussion consume much time. Often, the amount of time necessary to allow good interpersonal relationships to develop is not available to problem solvers in business and government. Practical considerations cannot be ignored for them. The discussion group in business and government is required to produce a solution, regardless of how well the members get along. Their method of operation is dictated by the requirements of the problem, not the personal needs of group members. What the group **must** do is controlled by the external demands of conditions that must be remedied. The behavior of members is incidental. Every effort should be made to protect the rights, privileges, and feelings of group members, but given a choice between a logical decision that may hurt feelings and an illogical one that would result in interpersonal harmony, the former must be selected. It is hard to do this without a method for adjudication. PERT is precisely such a method. It is a referee that determines whether the demands of the question have been met. Disgruntled members may vent their spleen against impartial statistics if they wish.

Emphasis on interaction and consensus tends to minimize harmful conflict. Sometimes, however, groups may be so zealous about avoiding conflict that they select an inadequate or ineffective solution merely because they can agree on it. If constructive interaction is not sufficient to produce a satisfactory solution, PERT requires the group to find something workable, like it or not.

PERT-based discussion is not antagonistic to constructive interpersonal dynamics, nor does it block creativity and imagination. Imposing a PERT base on problem solving merely focuses attention of the members on output rather than on their personal relations. Since they have a clear-cut goal, they are less likely to quarrel about what their job really is. Consensus is necessary in all the discussion steps leading to the PERT analysis, but awareness of PERT's requirements tends to minimize specious disagreements that impede consensus. PERT helps translate consensus into action. Group activity is sustained beyond the solution stage, so that the skill and knowledge of members can be applied to operations planning. What was previously an administrative matter now uses the group to make decisions.

PERT planning, discovery of events, drawing the network, listing activities, etc., are group processes very much like those that led to the solution the group is trying to make operational. The group is merely working on a new topic, "What can be done to carry out the solution we have agreed on?" Each step of the PERT process depends on the information, skills, and insights of the members. The term "collective wisdom" is not facetiously applied to PERT. After a group has worked through a problem, they develop an insight, a "feeling" for the problem, that no administrator could approximate. There are subtleties in their solution which are reflections of the group's experience. The executive may ignore these in his implementation, but if he does so he materially reduces the effectiveness of the solution. Use of the group to develop the operations plan means that administrative whim is less likely to nullify the group's work.

One hazard in group problem solving is the way people seem to get preoccupied with words. Sometimes, it seems, they feel that if they could discover a magic formula, the problems of the world would go away; if only they could agree on the right terminology, they would have found the right action. We can solve the problem of war by "disarmament," which would come about ". . . if all the nations in the world would recognize that it is to their best interest to disarm." Nations don't do that, though, not the way the group wants them to, so that the solution is impossible. A PERT plan would indicate this immediately when b time for the Soviet Union's disarmament was set at infinity. We can solve the problems of race hatred, delinquency, and poverty with "education." In small groups, the desire to "educate" ranks with the desire to "eliminate sin" among the ministry. The word "educate" is far from a specific educational program with precise goals, directed toward solution of a particular problem. Education is a vague abstraction if it is not accompanied by specific statements about who will be educated about what, and by whom. Reading Horace or Cicero will not enable a young, unemployed father in Appalachia to develop skills that will help him find a job in another location. Education about how desirable it might be "to live together as neighbors" does not seem to alter, materially, the tendency of white persons to close off their neighborhoods to nonwhites. Ordinances and specific programs might accomplish the objective, even though they might stir up a little conflict along the way. Groups must bring forth concrete solutions if they are to live up to their obligations and avoid "solution voodoo."

Another problem inherent in the group process is the frustration that comes with failure. The group process is not infallible. It does not always guarantee a good solution, or, for that matter, any solution at all. It is hard to go back over ground already covered, knowing that things did not work out well on the first try. Yet it cannot be assumed that every group will solve every problem on the first try. Any solution is capable of being unrealistic, unworkable, not pertinent to the problem. Group members must recognize the possibility of failure and be willing to subject their work to logical tests. PERT is a format by which a group can check their work, and if failure seems likely, they can determine the point at which they went wrong. They need not start all over again. Their frustration is not so great because, after all, they have saved something from their original labors. Alterations in the PERT diagram may force the group to go back through all the steps they have covered, but they do this in the framework of a method. This is part of their game of problem solving. The group need not have a mind-set for failure on the second try, if they have a methodology to prepare them to act appropriately when failure appears imminent.

PERT is a realistic method applied to the discussion process which tends to preserve the constructive elements of traditional problem solving, while adding a new dimension of emphasis on discussion output.

FIVE

Human relations in the small group

There is a common fallacy about small groups, that there is an optimum way to behave to ensure effective participation. It is questionable whether there is an optimum technique for any behavior, and in discussion, "one man's meat is another's poison." A man can talk a lot in one group and find himself made leader. He can try the same thing with other people and find himself excoriated for being a troublemaker. The quiet man is sometimes regarded with respect, almost as a sage, and sometimes ignored entirely. Behavior in the small group must be adjusted to the small group. The soundest caution is, the member should integrate his personality into the group as best he can, without losing his identity. Presumably, if each member sacrifices something of himself to the group, discussion will afford a proper synthesis of intelligence, creativity, and values, and the consensus will be truly representative.

If there is any personal trait that can be generally encouraged in discussion, it is willingness. The effective participant in small groups is the one who is willing to say something when it is necessary to say something, without getting personally identified with his remarks. Participation without advocacy is what is wanted. No person is capable of evaluating his own remarks objectively. The discussion member transmits his ideas to the group, to let them examine and evaluate them and their potential use to the group, and he must do this without offering a partisan defense. It seems to be a tall order for any mortal man. To adopt the attitude of, "I think this idea is worthwhile or I wouldn't offer it, but it's up to you to determine what to make of it," may be an ideal, but it is apparently unattainable for most of us.

Sometimes it is all we can do to remain in the group, everyone seems so hostile. It is not hard to get the idea that it really isn't worth the effort to talk because everything you say will be squelched. Still, there is some reason to believe that if one man feels this way, there might be another man who shares his feeling. The man who thinks he is a minority of one ought, at least, to try to advance an idea tentatively and watch how quickly someone else picks it up. The self-designated minority of one may turn out to be the future style leader of the group. Enlightened self-interest in the group demands participation to a reasonable extent, and at least suppression of the outward signs of the natural hostility evoked by criticism of remarks.

Somehow, deviant opinions must be encouraged also. It has been demonstrated that minority ideas can influence the thinking of majorities. Sometimes people believe the way they do because they have never heard anything else. Contact between majority and minority ideas is the material out of which consensus is built. Sulking in silent opposition is not useful either to member or group. The member may find that stomach turbulance is the result of bottling up his ideas. The group is denied the use of a possibly worthwhile contribution. If members can, somehow, get the idea that the best group is one made up of a seething ferment of ideas, some of the personal fears and threats can be dropped and true co-operative efforts can be made to achieve a discussion goal.

The interaction game[1]

People tend to develop patterns in their personal communications. As they speak to others, they begin to expect certain responses in

[1] When this section was being drafted, the writer had just encountered an "obscure" little book by Eric Berne called **Games People Play** (New York: Grove Press, 1964). By the time the final draft was being composed, it had become a best seller. It is recommended as the source of the idea for this section and as something well worth reading in its own right because of the way it penetrates to the core of human transaction.

return. In turn, their own conversation becomes stylized, forming a pattern for their protagonist. Standardized interactions lead to expectancies in the communication. Failure in expectations leads to breakdown of communications. Standardized verbal responses in which there are regular moves in response to regular moves can be referred to as "the interaction game."

Communication in a small group can be understood as a multi-player game, according to Berne's definition of game as "an ongoing series of complementary, ulterior transactions progressing to a well-defined outcome." Games need not be fun, as ice hockey is not fun for the participants, sometimes. The distinguishing feature of a human game is its conformance to rules and expectations of the participants.

There are both constructive and destructive games that can be played in discussion. A game begins with a standard statement made by a member of a group. Another member responds. If he responds as expected, the game is usually played out to its finish. If a constructive game has been started, the group will make progress. If a destructive game has been introduced, the group will bog down or hit a snag. There are an infinite number of verbal games possible, but some occur more frequently than others. Following are some recurrent games to be found played in small groups.

"Let's co-operate." This game is opened by one member saying, "I know there are some fundamental differences here, but what are the things we can agree on?" If a second member offers a concrete suggestion, the group is off to a good start. Establishing a series of agreements helps the group to set itself for future agreement and permits constructive resolution of whatever conflict occurs. Sometimes, however, the game is overplayed and the group reaches a sham agreement early in the discussion, only to have it break apart when the solution stage is reached.

"Let's Co-operate" must be refereed carefully by the group leader, who should play his own game of, ". . . but there's something you may not have taken into account!" The leader's game is to introduce material that might cast doubt on the authenticity of agreements, to be sure that conflict has not been glossed over by verbalizations.

A variant of "Let's Co-operate" is "Sweet Reason." This game is opened when someone wants to break up a conflict. The player will suggest that "men of goodwill can find a way out." He may even make suggestions about the "way." If played by a leader with high status in the group, the game is helpful. If introduced by a rejected member, he may find himself the focal point of argument, with all of the contending parties turning their wrath on him in resentment at his interruption of their "Battle."

The basic rule of "Let's Co-operate" is the obvious and visible suppression of disagreements in order to find agreements. A winning player will significantly broaden the base of understanding in the group. A losing player will find that he has helped to construct a series of counterfeit agreements and raise the potential for trouble when it is time to agree on a solution.

"I want my way!" This game disrupts the group. A basic assumption of most small-group discussants is that members will be somewhat problem-centered and goal-oriented, able to submerge a bit of themselves into what the group is doing. In proceeding toward a group goal, necessity, rather than desire, is the most practical criterion for decisions. Communication is often directed to disseminating the idea that there is a way better than others and it is up to the group to find it, regardless of what may appear to be desirable to any member at the moment. The "I Want My Way!" player refuses to accept this sort of reasoning and demands that his ideas be accepted, no matter what.

When played by an authoritarian leader, the group is quickly whipped into line. In business discussions, for example, where the leader is also the man who signs the paychecks, any signal from him of "I Want My Way!" sets off a game of "We Hear and Obey, Master" among the other players. The individual who wants to play "I Disagree" is likely to suffer sanctions outside of the discussion, and he knows it. He may play his game out of sincere conviction, or he may play because he wanted to look for another job anyway.

At best, the game of "I Want My Way!" delays decision making. When the game is opened, the rest of the members must pay reasonable attention, and a complex game of "Let's Co-operate" must be played to redirect the deviant player back into the group. More often, a game of "Conflict" develops and if the group is not strong enough, the "I Want My Way!" player may gradually pick up allies and win his point. If the group cannot recover and overturn decisions made while under the influence of "I Want My Way!" the quality of the solution suffers accordingly.

"It can't be done." "It Can't Be Done" is best introduced at two points in the discussion. The most effective disruption point is just after the group has reached agreement on the nature and extent of their problem. The "It Can't Be Done" player presents a tightly reasoned argument showing how "even the best minds of our generation have not succeeded in solving this problem," and "this group is even more limited in resources than any previous group." The inescapable conclusion is that everyone should give up and go home.

The second critical point is after someone has proposed a solution. The "It Can't Be Done" player comes forward with a barrage of reasons why the proposal is impossible. This use of the game often is constructive, particularly if the group has come up with an excessively hazy solution. The "It Can't Be Done" game helps identify meaningless proposals and motivates greater precision in presentation of ideas.

"Let's get on with it." "Let's Get On With It" is a constructive game for the most part. When played by an impatient member, however, the group may be hurried to the point where they ignore major issues and end up with a perfunctory solution.

A constructive player opens his game when another member of the group has started a game of "This Is Dull, Let's Talk about Something Else." The "Let's Get On with It" player reminds the group that they have a purpose and that the present activity is extraneous. The opening move should include a suggestion about how to get on with it.

It is helpful to the leader if a member starts the game so that he (the leader) can lend support without appearing to be exerting pressure himself. If there is only one player, the group can conveniently ignore him and go on with their digression, but if there is more than one, including the leader, the group may be embarrassed back to discussion continuity.

"Battle" and "conflict." "Battle" is quite different from "Conflict." "Conflict" is played when several members legitimately disagree about the meaning of a fact or the implications of an idea. The group game provides for resolution of "Conflict" in its rules. The leader or a member may present fresh information, inject new ideas, or seek consensus in other ways. "Battle" starts when a player decides he is going to play "King of the Hill" and defend his remarks against all comers because anyone who opposes his ideas opposes him as well. The first move in "Battle" is to take offense at some comment about the player's previous remark. The object of hostility retaliates with a personal attack. "Battle" players must be careful to avoid saying anything at all pertinent to the discussion. Remarks must be confined entirely to personalities in order to get a good, hot game going.

Few people can resist the challenge to "Battle." As soon as there are two "Battle" players, a game of "Team Battle" can be started by choosing up sides. Each nasty remark directed against a member puts him on the other side. Sometimes the team game converges on the two original players, with the others contributing personal attacks on the starters. Sometimes "Team Battle" can turn into "Anarchy" if various members pair off to play their own game all at the same time.

Hopefully, the group leader, at least, will stay out of it and try to get the group to play "Let's Get On with It" or at least "Conflict." If he gets embroiled himself, there is little hope. Most of what the leader can do to stop a "Battle" game is ineffective. He can assume an authoritarian role and demand that the players stop. If he has high prestige and has not tried it too often, he may be able to pull it off and get the game broken up. He may then try observer-feedback to show the group what happened. If he can get the group to accept role playing, it will probably reveal the absurdity of the game. Unless he can get the group to sit quietly for a while, both of these devices will fail. Whatever he does, he must do it quickly. The longer a game of "Battle" is allowed to go on, the less likely it is that the group can survive it.

"This is dull, let's talk about something else." It's a rare member who can resist an occasional whirl at "This Is Dull." It is normally a harmless game. The longer a discussion goes on, the harder the chairs seem to get. It's hard to sit still. A little diversion is necessary. Simple boredom can induce a member to start "This Is Dull" by telling a story. This can set off a game of "Can You Top This?" or "Show and Tell" in which each player offers his own pet story. Discussion, of course, stops while this is going on. Periodic short games of "This Is Dull" tend to refresh the group, so long as they do not last too long, though some observers testify that if a "This Is Dull" game is allowed to run its course, members will return to the discussion in self-defense, finding it considerably less dull than the story hour. The leader must be alert for an appropriate time to interrupt the game. Customarily he waits until one or two people have made their moves and then introduces "Let's Get On with It." Most "This Is Dull" players are perfectly willing to quit when they discover they've already heard the stories.

"What do YOU want?" "What Do YOU Want?" is sometimes known as the game of "Alphonse and Gaston." It is played by two people, each attempting to be more gracious than the other by refusing to give their opinion until the other one has gone first. The purpose is to find an opportunity to agree magnanimously with the other player's ideas. A variant is played as "Oh My, You Know So Much More About It Than I Do" by a member who is really not prepared for the discussion but wants to build a reputation as a co-operator.

Overzealousness about the "ideals" of the discussion process motivates many games of "What Do YOU Want?" Some participants feel that they have no obligation at all to present their own ideas and spend their time trying to find ideas to agree with.

Etc. There are probably as many games as there are group members. Groups are well advised to examine their own games and attempt to avoid destructive ones. This can be done simply by refusing to return the expected response to the initiating player. Later in this chapter we will discuss the consequences of the entire group getting involved in a game and offer some suggestions about how to identify a group that has failed and what to do about it.

The special case of the hidden agenda[2]

The phrase "hidden agenda" refers to the personal, idiosyncratic goals and feelings that individuals bring with them into a group discussion. These personal goals can interfere with achievement of group goals. An understanding of the relationship between personal goals and group goals assists in gaining understanding of how people behave in discussion.

Hidden agendas are not necessarily malicious or even conscious attempts to disrupt the group process. Most of the time, members are not even aware when they are acting on a hidden agenda. They may honestly feel that they are co-operating to the best of their ability. Exercise of empathy confers insight into the potential influence of personal goals on discussion outcomes. Since no one can be

---

[2]The phrase "hidden agenda" was originated by Leland Bradford in an article, "The Case of the Hidden Agenda," **Adult Leadership** (September 1952). It has since become part of the vocabulary of those who deal with small groups.

expected to discard his personality when he enters a group, the group should experience considerable behavior motivated by hidden agendas. There are four main sources.

Physical problems. We are prisoners of our physiology. A great deal of human behavior occurs because of physical feelings. A person who is uncomfortable may disturb the harmony of the group. A severe headache might impel a member to work urgently toward a premature solution in order to get home to take an aspirin. If a member seems to be acting in disruptive fashion, it should not be assumed that he is doing so out of a desire to sabotage the work of the group. An attempt should be made to see if he becomes more co-operative after his physical needs are attended to. Sometimes it is helpful to excuse him graciously from the discussion.

People are often so quick to evaluate the behavior of others that they lose sight of the simplest explanation. It is prudent to discover whether some simple physiological need may be motivating hostile behavior before attempting a complex personality analysis. For example, lack of fresh air and uncomfortable chairs can cause much surliness. Care should be taken to meet minimum standards of comfort in the discussion room. People respond differently to discomfort, but generally all need light, air, comfortable chairs, and a good place to put their feet and lay down their notes. Ash trays should be provided and periodic breaks taken for relaxation and refreshment. Restlessness and impatience may be signs of impending conflict within the group. They may also be signs of physical discomfort. Since many of the conditions leading to physical discomfort can be easily remedied, this matter should not be left to chance.

Concern for group role. Mutual respect makes good relations easier. No member wants his contributions denigrated. One who is "sensitive" may read personal hostilities into the simplest expression of criticism by another member. Consistent devaluation of his opinions may force a member to take the role of chronic dissenter in which he objects to everything, anticipating rejection, but feeling the need to strike back at the group.

This is not a conscious process. The member will not know why he is behaving as he is. Members rarely make a direct attempt to disturb interaction because of real or imagined slights. Indeed, such action would be a sign of paranoia. However, human beings do respond to evaluative cues from others. Polite verbal acceptance associated with nonverbal messages that could be classified as "rejecting" tends to push a member into a position where he feels hostility to the group enterprise is what is expected of him. He replies in kind.

Honest mutual respect tends to alleviate this kind of hidden agenda. A permissive atmosphere in which remarks are accepted by all tends to make individuals feel part of the group. This does not imply the abandonment of criticism, but does mean that members take care to direct remarks at contributions not contributors. Gentle response is preferable to direct attack in assisting the member with a personality-based hidden agenda in abandoning it gracefully. Authoritarian methods may prompt rebellion or, at best, truculent assent. In some cases, agreements are wrecked in later stages of discussion because an individual felt rejection earlier and is responding to his internal feelings of hostility.

Members should not be forced into an advocate's role. Overreaction should be guarded against. If a member presents an idea in an appropriately tentative way only to have it subjected to unwarranted attack, he may respond with hostility before investigating the reasons for the attack. He may feel legitimately threatened and become defensive, forgetting temporarily the proper orientation to discussion. Overreaction of this sort tends to leave permanent scars, capable of splitting the group into hostile factions.

Everyone prefers to retain his individuality and self-respect despite the fact that he is a group member. When a member feels excluded, he will try to regain his prestige through co-operation. If this fails, hostility is the most logical alternative. The group should co-operate to preserve the integrity of each member.

External loyalties. External loyalties are another source of hidden agenda. Although a man is a group member at a given time, he retains loyalties from his other affiliations. His political, social, and religious commitments will affect his behavior. He will respond negatively to ideas which appear to jeopardize his basic beliefs.

Objections based on external loyalties should not be ignored. If the group tramples on the values and beliefs of its members, no consensus can result. If a member presents a point of view drastically different from that of the other members, it deserves careful examination, not abrupt dismissal. If a large number of people outside the group also hold the "unpopular" position, it may mean that the group's solution would be jeopardized if it failed to take them into account.

Hidden agenda based on external loyalties can be conducive to consensus, if they can be made manifest. A group member influenced by the "Catholic" position should, for the moment, speak to his group as a representative of Catholicism. The group can decide if the view is truly representative. If it is, then they can revise their own views, if support from Catholics is essential to the success of their solution.

No member should be forced into a position where he is embarrassed by his external affiliations. Particularly in community problem-solving groups, which draw their members from all strata and segments of society, it is necessary to discuss controversy resulting from external loyalties and not permit them to grow into destructive forces which can tear the group apart.

Interpersonal developments. There is no way of predicting how a group of strangers called together to serve as a group will react to each other. Affinities and hostilities will develop for no apparent reason. Even selection based on sociometric choice is not infallible. Any contact between members, friends, enemies, or strangers may set off a chain of events that will develop into more or less permanent likes or hates, which in turn will influence the orientation of members toward the issues of the discussion.

A member who is antagonistic to another may unconsciously oppose anything he says, without fully appreciating his motivation. Hostility need not be mutual to be dangerous. In fact, mutual hostility is sometimes more constructive, for it is more likely to become overt conflict, which can be observed and controlled. Seething resentment because of a chance remark can develop into unidirected hostility capable of seriously disrupting the group.

Friendships function the same way. Members may be uncritical in supporting ideas because they happen to like the person that presented them. Particularly in student discussions, socially popular members have no trouble obtaining allies. Socially acceptable members will influence others to support their ideas in return for admission into a select social circle. Desire for approval by leaders may motivate undiscriminating assent by members who want social approval more than they want to achieve the group goal.

The personality of group members exerts a pronounced influence on the group. The goal should be concordance between individual goals and those of the group, recognizing that complete sublimation of personality is neither possible nor desirable. It is, in fact, the clash of diverse personalities that provides the constructive essence of group problem solving. Synthesis or consensus implies difference to begin with. If there is unanimity of opinion at the outset, then the group becomes an authoritarian entity and tends to precipitate out anyone who threatens the established group creed. The group purpose then becomes mutual self-support. The various "anti-Communist study groups" are examples of groups with worthwhile goals that concentrate on obtaining only members who are entirely in accord with their methods and ideas. This procedure eliminates the possibility of self-correction and results in the dissemination of dogma rather than the solution of problems. Differences in views as well as differences in style of expression should be encouraged in order to achieve a stronger consensus.

Common reasons for failure of groups

Problem-solving groups, educational groups, therapeutic groups, and social groups often fail: sometimes by accident, sometimes on purpose. They may not be clear about what is expected of them. They may assume that their job is simply to find agreement, whether it makes sense or not. They may decide that they have to seek the one "true and good" solution, and then agree that they can't find it. Some group members may regard the discussion as a contest between their side and the "wrong side" in which the goal is victory. There are only a few rational souls who come into discussion regarding it as a method of relating intelligently with other human beings so that one idea or solution may be selected from among the many possible.

The committee system is a microcosm through which the failures of the small group can be studied. It was remarked earlier that officers are "people who run for office so they can appoint the committees rather than serve on them." Anyone who is active in his school or community knows that committees are everywhere. Once such persons succumb to the urge to render service by helping to plan a paper sale or organize a P.T.A. bazaar, they are "hooked." It is even rumored that some organizations keep a list of committee-prone people to appoint to all manner of committees. That is why it seems like the same people are always doing all the work.

College faculty members bemoan their fate when they are called upon to serve on university committees and complain about "excessive work loads." They have not learned that the committee is the key to promotion. Students find committees to be the entrée to social prestige and campus power, at least among those students who know that the committees exist. In industry, committees may be called "planning groups" or by some other euphemism, but their function is essentially the same. In government, one authority calculated, there are more planning groups and committees than there are people on the government payroll. The recent rise in government employees' salaries is probably "hardship pay" for the time they have to spend on committees.

It is hard to learn how to behave on a committee. Members often have no clear idea of what constitutes success or failure. Agreement on a series of verbalizations does not constitute success. A feeling of tension and anxiety does not constitute failure. The words must have some meaning, the feelings must assist the meaning regardless of the type of group. Meaningful action is what is sought by problem solvers; educational-group members desire understanding; therapy-group members seek constructive behavior change.

Some typical pitfalls to group success are presented below, together with recommendations about how to avoid them. Critical awareness of what the group is doing is most helpful; the member who can contribute constructive ideas about improvement of the group's process is a most valuable asset. Not all the possible methods of failure are catalogued here. Each group must diagnose itself.

The method of the widespread solution. It is easy for committees to evade responsibility by showing that their problem is beyond their ability to solve. A P.T.A. group discussing delinquency in its district might agree that "Delinquency is characteristic of our modern day and a symptom of fundamental disturbance in our society." A management committee could reach consensus on "The problem of utilizing cybernetic methods in office management pervades the industry of our time. Any methods proposed for this company are dependent on the method eventually adopted by business in general." The faculty approach might be: "Accommodation of greater numbers of students is a problem plaguing all colleges and cannot be solved on our campus alone." Finally, the students might agree: "The dwindling of student government is only part of the more general problem of apathy characteristic of our day."

None of these statements is really a solution. Delinquency would persist in the school district; the company would continue to use outmoded office equipment; students would come to campus and find no housing; and hardly anyone would vote in the next student election.

Solutions with so little impact signify that consensus was about the words in the report. The groups really worked on the problem, "How should our report be worded?" They paid little attention to real activities designed to solve problems. Saying solution words may make members feel good, but their report offers little help or encouragement to anyone really affected by the problem.

Even if a problem is widespread and the causes cannot be dealt with, it is still possible to propose and apply symptomatic solutions. Groups should not be disconcerted when they find that fundamental causes often are beyond their scope. If they have decided, for example, that "delinquency begins in the home and is a symptom of family failure," they can still direct solutions at families in their local community by setting up foster homes or providing jobs for breadwinners. They need not try to solve the problem on all levels. A look at their scope of authority would tell them this was impossible, anyway.

Any statement of cause should have been built from an examination of specifics. Returning attention to specifics helps the group avoid the discouragement that comes from confronting an excessively broad problem. When members show signs of such loss of confidence, questions about the possibility of local solutions can help to salvage the spirit of the group.

In educational discussions, care taken at the definition phase will enable the group to work on something reasonable. It is probably unlikely that they would ever come to agreement on a statement evaluating **all** of Hemingway or explaining the cause of **all** poverty. Phases of the problems can be dealt with conveniently.

Excessive idealism. When dealing with remote issues, it is simple to take an idealistic approach and agree on a proposal that overreaches the power of the group. When problem solvers dealing with real issues do this, the result is a solution that is worthless because it so far exceeds the capabilities of administration as to be incapable of execution.

For example, students might report, "This committee declares that our student government should convince every other student government in the land that they should support the overseas education program." The P.T.A. solution might read, "This citizen's committee will root out pornography wherever it is found in this land of ours." The academicians sum up their discussion with "The academic committee proposes a plan to produce well-rounded men and women educated around a classical core, and capable of taking their proper place in a technological society." The experts of industry show their wisdom with "Our program is designed to take the market away from competition on every level."

Of course problem solvers should maintain an idealistic attitude. If they did not feel that a solution was possible, there would be no reason for them to come to the meeting. They must understand, however, that a reasonable solution involves the use of people and resources. A solution that exceeds the resources of the agency assigned to carry it out is an evasion of responsibility. The group member who suggests that it is better to succeed with some solution in a small way than to fail gloriously in attempting a grandiose solution should not be called a "petty-minded literalist" and ignored. Some suggestions for resisting excessive idealism include continually asking, "Will it work?" "Who will do it?" "How much will it cost?" For the examples given, a student might suggest that one member of the student group put up the money to finance a tour of the country to see if other campuses will agree. The P.T.A. group could be asked how the committee members would get to Honolulu to investigate pornography. (The person who asks the question might also volunteer to make the trip.) Someone could propose to the faculty that the most vocal members of the group leave the room and try to agree on a list of required courses. The ambitious salesmen might be interrogated about the closest competitor in a specific market.

Personality conflict threat. The literature on conflict in small groups is extensive enough to indicate either that conflict is present to greater or lesser degrees in all discussions or that there is some pathological preoccupation with conflict among researchers. The former is more likely to be the case. One of the greatest barriers to successful discussion is conflict about personalities.

Some examples:

> Community Group Member 1: There are 221 substandard homes in our community!
>
> Community Group Member 2: Mr. Smith says there are a lot less. You people better get your facts straight!

Or

> Professor 1: I believe this is our only recourse.
>
> Professor 2: I don't suppose you've heard what Dr. Jones thinks about your opinions.

Still another:

> Student 1: I don't think we can afford to ignore the faculty on this matter.
>
> Student 2: You fraternity men are like that, always trying to curry favor with the faculty.

Finally:

> Department Head 1: I think our department can get along with that budget.
>
> Department Head 2: So can we, but I can't help wondering why Smith's and Brown's departments are getting a 20 per cent increase while yours is only getting 10 per cent.

External loyalties, even if irrelevant, can be used to get two or more members embroiled in argument. In the student example, the issue of the worth of fraternities is not related to a discussion on relations with the faculty.

No employee can resist worrying about his position in the company. When somebody, supposedly equal, gets more, a real threat is posed. Getting people to quibble over facts, as in the first example, or gossip, as in the second, can trigger serious tensions between members. No one can become totally problem-centered, and it would be undesirable if they could, for this would mean a loss of identity. There must be a delicate balance achieved between the group and individual goals. It is easy for personality conflict to disrupt this balance.

Conflict can be made to work for the welfare of the group. Examination of motives of conflicting members often provides a clue to resolution. A dispute over facts, for example, can be resolved by examining sources or getting new information. An extraneous conflict can be broken up by laughter over the irrelevancy. Gossip fails, if it is ignored. The competitive urge can be suppressed by presenting good reasons why one man is treated differently than another. Each type of disruption through personality conflict has its antidote, if leader and members move quickly. If the group settles on a pattern of conflict, consensus may be impossible. If someone can get the group into habits of co-operation, conflict can be resisted.

Frank expression of hidden agendas helps to prevent harmful conflict, for example, in an "economic" conflict between fellow church members:

> One member declares that the new church could be built if every member of the fund-raising committee would start the ball rolling with a donation of $500. Those who have $500 think it a delightful idea and savor the prestige that would come from the grand gesture. Those who do not have $500 are reluctant to admit that they don't. Those who have assert, "This is the sort of thing that would really catch the attention of the congregation and motivate other big donations." Those who do not declare, "It would be embarrassing to some if their contributions were revealed, and anyway, church business should not be done this way."

Real heat can be generated until someone stops protecting his socio-economic position and simply admits he just doesn't have the money. This would dissipate the conflict and lead the group to explore other possible solutions.

There is nothing so frightening as an attack on someone's livelihood. If there are problems in a company department, someone might declare, "A new broom sweeps clean! Let's get a whole new crew." This makes the employees under attack defensive, more sensitive to criticism, and may embroil them in conflict with everyone else. If a truce can be obtained while ten or twelve other possible causes are pointed out, the potential conflict can be prevented.

Conflict over credos or verbal formulas is virtually impossible to understand, much less deal with. Disputes about the "local community" versus "the federal government" can generate considerable heat, but it is hard to pinpoint what fights like these are about. Cultural conditioning inculcates slogans very deeply into our personalities, and involvement with belief-words is very strong. About the only hope is prevention, keeping the group's attention on factual material and keeping them diverted from abstractions. Saying the problem in words that refer to things that can be seen (or at least documented) prevents the need for dramatic slogans. Questions like local versus federal government need never come up if the group stays focused on a real problem. If members begin to quarrel about deep-seated values, the group is in real trouble. Conflicts started long before the members came into the group will not be resolved in a transitory situation; indeed, they are likely to persist long after the group goes out of existence. In such cases, the only hope is temporary amelioration, long enough to do what is necessary. There is little point in attempting to settle philosophical issues in thirty minutes that took years to develop. Symptomatic treatment of the immediate conditions usually will result in some agreement, and the group is not a total failure.

Discussion without some conflict is dull. Groups sometimes get involved in harmful conflict without even being fully aware of what they are doing. In order to prevent such conflict from becoming habit forming, someone, usually the leader, must effect a resolution at once.

Effective leadership is the best antidote for harmful conflict. Problem-centered controversy about legitimate issues can be constructively resolved. This kind of conflict is essential, for if agreement is too easily reached, consensus may be superficial. Personality conflict is the group's most severe threat. Leadership is both an art and a skill calling for knowledge of the group process and of the behavior of human beings. Without this, the leader can only be inept as he tries to deal with conflict. The leader who can handle it is the group's most valuable asset and the surest defense against disruption.

Finding the least common denominator. Groups who wish to avoid conflict at all costs (including no solution) can find a way out by seeking a minimum statement that all members can agree on, and calling it a solution. Examples:

The businessmen: "Both sides agree that something must be done about seeing to it that meals are available at lunchtime." (The issue was employee benefits.)

The students, discussing Spring Week: "Then we're agreed that it should be some time after mid-terms."

Community leader discussing P.T.A. policy toward the proposed teacher pay increase: ". . . it should be commensurate with the needs of both the teachers and the taxpayers."

The faculty approach to revising required courses: "We agree that the courses required should represent a sampling of the humanities, sciences, and social sciences, but not quantitatively severe enough to impair sound vocational training, with the understanding that the student must have time for personal growth."

There are two basic approaches: trivia and nebulosity. The trivial approach is most effective, for if the agreement is announced with sufficient fanfare, the public will be impressed and ask for nothing more. It is similar to what the impression would have been in October 1964 if newspapers had headlined, "Goldwater and Johnson Agree!" Few would have read on to discover that both men had responded to an athletic-club questionnaire and agreed that the President should throw out the first ball at the opening game of the baseball season.

The nebulosity approach is artistic, because it sometimes creates statements like: "We oppose prejudice wherever it may be found and call on men of goodwill to eliminate this poison from their hearts and minds!" Measuring the productivity of a discussion group by the quantity of agreement reached is somewhat like determining the winner of a football game by counting first downs. Advocates of the "least-common-denominator" consensus are often men of "goodwill" who sincerely believe that agreement is more important than a workable solution. In order to avoid ruffled feelings, they might agree that unicorns were real. Pity the hunting expedition that went out seeking the unicorns because of that solution.

The fact that people like to finish makes the least-common-denominator approach so deadly. Once the "solution" is agreed on, the members can congratulate each other and go home. They might feel only a little guilty when asked, "Will it work?"

A good way to identify a least-common-denominator solution is to look for some key words: "education," "moral," "religious," "patriotic," "every man," and "duty." Emphasis is heavy on "education." When advocates of an education-type solution are asked specific questions, they reply, "We'll leave that to the experts. After all, we regard teachers as professionals." Who can argue with that (besides the educators who are handed another program they don't quite know what to do with)? The trivia variant is also obvious. An outsider looks at the final report and says, "Is this all?" The group can answer, "We worked three months on our report and it represents our true consensus!"

Antidotes to the least-common-denominator problem:

To the businessmen: Keep asking "What else?" "What about the pension problem?" "What about the vacation problem?" and most useful of all, "What shall I tell the newspaper people when I see them this evening?"

To the students: Say, "We don't get the **money** until we file the date, time, and place in the dean's office."

To the P.T.A.: Although you might be tempted to say "Baloney," or "That's a big help," it might be useful to volunteer to head a committee to report on teacher and taxpayer needs. Hardly anyone will show up when you give your report, and you might get your own way.

To the faculty: Declare "Fine, I guess that means we require two courses in my subject. I'll write that down."

Defense of the status quo. There's an element of risk in problem solving—the solution might not work. Sometimes it is even more frightening to contemplate what might happen if it did. For this reason, many members tend to cling to the present and attempt to justify it in spite of its defects. The defense takes a fairly consistent form:

"The present program is the result of the painstaking labors of the men and women who have gone before us. With all its defects, it represents the optimum program," or

"We have surveyed several proposals and find that potential problems inherent in each are far more severe than our present problems. We are prepared to accept our present difficulties in preference to risking . . ." (Here fill in as gloomy a set of prospects as possible.)

A subtle twist is the "modified status quo": "Any problem we now face can be handled by modifications in our present program. What is really needed is faith and support for our administrators."

The defense of the status quo is materially assisted by the feeling many members have that they are expected to come up with something totally new. They fear the consequences of radical changes and are not aware that they are permitted to build an eclectic solution. The counterpart of the status quo defense is the "Bold New Program." In this operation, the group decides that everything presently being done must be scrapped and that they must "start from scratch." They can evade a solution by asking for more time and additional resources. If they report out minor portions of their "Bold New Program," they can please liberals and conservatives alike. Liberals wait patiently for the program. Conservatives are delighted that nothing much seems to be happening.

The antidote is fairly simple to apply. Merely keep inquiring about specific problems. Ask how the present program is handling the problem. If someone tells you to have "faith," ask "In whom or what?" Keep asking. Keep making it clear that even the best programs can use some adjustments as conditions change.

Veneration of research. Problem solvers sometimes take refuge by lingering at the fact-finding stage. There are a number of devices used:

> Report A: "The committee finds the problem so complex that it feels that a special fact-finding committee should be appointed to study the problem in depth."
>
> Report B: "The committee is currently conducting research on the question and will hold the report in abeyance until satisfied that the situation is understood."
>
> Report C: "We cannot present a report until all the facts are in."

In the first report, the clever twist, of course, is that the original committee was appointed to do precisely what they ask the new committee to do. The process can be extended **ad infinitum** because each request for a new committee serves as a report. Everyone seems to be satisfied that something is happening, except the few people who need a solution to the problem.

The second variation is especially appropriate today when research is so important. If a problem-solving group decides to do research instead of solving a problem, everyone will be very pleased. Financing is easy to obtain and the group can be sustained for years doing very little.

The third report can postpone a decision permanently. With things changing so fast, the committee will never get **all** the facts. The report sounds so sincere, however, that hardly anyone will question it.

Antidotes:

> Announce: "Listen, we can ask for the new committee but it's got to be **quid pro quo** (the use of Latin is always impressive). Let's give the folks a partial solution anyway." This may get something going when the group discovers that a solution is not really impossible.

Try: "Right! Let's get a committee to write a proposal so we can get it financed." Suggest the members who used the word "research" most often. Then say, "The rest of us will try to muddle through while they're working on the proposal." Surprisingly enough, the group may even succeed in muddling through to a solution be- fore the proposal committee even gets off the ground. The only response to the man who wants to wait for all the facts is to suggest that he wait and let the group know when he has them. The rest can move on.

The refusal to complete. Problem-solving discussion is an orderly process that starts with a problem and ends with a solution that works. If the group avoids the implications of its solutions, it has probably wasted its time. It is not sufficient to stop with a list of goals or a general solution. A specific proposal is necessary, and a plan to carry it out is most useful. Attention should be paid to the needs of the members of the group, although such attention carried to extremes may divert the group from concern for the problem area.

That healthy interpersonal relations will improve the process of the group has been well documented. What is not sufficiently under- stood is that process can improve interpersonal relations. The proc- ess, or agenda, is the method through which people become problem- centered.

The development of an operations plan has been proposed as an intrinsic part of problem solving. It is the logical step after consen- sus on the solution. There is no more appropriate person or agency to originate the plan than the group that has developed the solution. PERT and related methods have been suggested as simple and direct applications for such planning. They depend on group co-operation. They utilize maximum talent and information of the members. Suffi- cient precision and form is imposed on the group so that it becomes easy for members to modify their personal agenda to fit the group goal. Discussion groups employing PERT derive a greater satisfaction from solving problems, for they know they have a good probability that their solution is workable, logical, and efficient, and hopefully can solve at least part of the problem.

When well done, there is really very little that can impair the dis- cussion process. Sophistication in methodology, understanding of potentials and limitations, and willingness to play the game are all demanded for success. Regrettably, many people who employ the process play at it. They are not adequately trained in technique or theory.

It is interesting to note what one well-trained person can do for a group. If he is not overeager and he moves with moderation, he can train the members in discussion while they discuss. The method is so logical and reasonable that simple exposure is the best pedagogical device.

Selected bibliography

Footnotes have been provided in the text where appropriate. Rather than impede the reader's progress through the text with unnecessary notes, some suggestions about worthwhile readings are offered. These do not necessarily represent the author's sources of material. They have been selected because they add depth and explication to the material covered. For the most part, they will be useful to the student, although some may appeal only to the student who is highly motivated and highly intelligent. The literature of small groups is not simple. The genuine student finds himself immersed in the literature of many fields: psychology, sociology, psychiatry, education, business, mathematics, and speech. Perhaps the works listed below are mainly useful for their bibliographies, which can be used to get the truly interested student started on a lifelong study.

Chapter One. An excellent general work on the nature of the small group is Michael Olmsted, **The Small Group** (New York: Random House, 1959). It is a thorough, yet simple treatment of origins of groups, their nature, behavior, function, and structure. It provides a bibliography of traditional source material. A more scholarly approach is Bronislaw Malinowski, "The Group and the Individual in Functional Analysis" (Indianapolis and New York: Bobbs-Merrill Reprint Series in the Social Sciences, No. 183). This work is a classic discourse on the relationship between individual and group.

An understanding of the function of groups in a democracy may be obtained from Franklyn S. Haiman, **Group Leadership and Demo-**

cratic Action (Boston: Houghton Mifflin, 1957). A good early study of
formation of natural groups is Grace L. Coyle, **Group Work with American Youth** (New York: Harper, 1948), and a discussion of the extent
to which groups have permeated industry and a discussion of the
ways in which they operate can be found in John Perry, **Human
Relations in Small Industry** (New York: McGraw-Hill, 1954). An excellent treatment of consensus may be found in Edith Becker Bennett,
"Discussion, Decision, Commitment and Consensus in Group Decision" (Indianapolis and New York: Bobbs-Merrill Reprint Series in the
Social Sciences, No. P271).

Two excellent examples of the type of approach taken by early
writers on group discussion are Henry Lee Ewbank and J. Jeffrey
Auer, **Discussion and Debate** (New York: Appleton-Century-Crofts,
1951), and James H. McBurney and Kenneth G. Hance, **Discussion in
Human Affairs** (New York: Harper, 1950). So influential were these
two books that the subsequent dozens of books written on group discussion after them varied only slightly in their treatment of technique
and almost not at all in their consideration of goals and objectives.

Chapter Two. Discussion of influences of group size and problem
type may be found in virtually any standard modern discussion text.
A particularly good one is R. Victor Harnack and Thorrel B. Fest,
Group Discussion: Theory and Technique (New York: Appleton-Century-Crofts, 1964). For an understanding of influence of personality
type refer to David Riesman **et al., The Lonely Crowd,** abridged ed.
(Garden City: Doubleday Anchor, 1953). Another good general discussion of communication and personality type may be found in Jurgen
Ruesch, **Therapeutic Communication** (New York: Norton, 1961). This
book also deals with possible consequences of disturbed communications among persons with personality disorders.

Perhaps the best consideration of leadership, in this writer's opinion, is in Franklyn Haiman, **Group Leadership and Democratic Action,**
referred to above. Haiman provides a thorough discussion of leadership sources, techniques and functions of leadership, and the role of
leadership in a democracy, with emphasis on problem-solving and
educational discussion. An approach to leadership from the stand-
point of therapy is Thomas Gordon, **Group-centered Leadership** (Boston: Houghton Mifflin, 1955). Gordon discusses a general therapy of
leadership in the therapy group, the goals of leadership, and some
simple techniques applicable to common forms of group therapy.

There is a great deal of material on interpersonal communication patterns in small groups. Two of the best can be found in the Bobbs-Merrill Reprint Series in the Social Sciences (Indianapolis and New York): Alex Bavelas, "Communication Patterns in Task-oriented Groups" (No. P25), and Theodore M. Newcomb, "An Approach to the Study of Communicative Acts" (No. P261). Bavelas' work is a pioneer study of communication networks. Newcomb considers a mathematical approach to communication patterns.

Further information about research styles can be obtained from any of the four standard compendia of small-group studies: Barry E. Collins and Harold Guetzkow, **A Social Psychology of Group Processes for Decision Making** (New York, Wiley, 1964), Robert T. Golembiewski, **The Small Group** (Chicago: The University of Chicago Press, 1962), A. Paul Hare, **Handbook of Small Group Research** (New York: The Free Press, 1962), or either edition of Dorwin Cartwright and Alvin Zander, **Group Dynamics: Research and Theory** (New York: Row, Peterson, 1953, or Evanston: Row, Peterson, 1960). Another work that can be examined for greater depth is Robert F. Bales, "A Set of Categories for the Analysis of Small Group Interaction" (Indianapolis and New York: Bobbs-Merrill Reprint Series in the Social Sciences, No. 5). This is the early article published by Bales on interactionist theory. A good example of mathematical model making is Robert F. Bales, Fred L. Strodtbeck, Theodore Mills, and Mary E. Roseborough, "Channels of Communication in Small Groups" (Indianapolis and New York: Bobbs-Merrill Reprint Series in the Social Sciences, No. 6).

Chapter Three. The literature on discussion in education and therapy is extensive. A basic work in education on the college level is Randall W. Hoffman and Robert Plutchik, **Small Group Discussion in Orientation and Teaching** (New York: Putnam, 1959). The authors describe their approach to the discussion method in the orientation of college students and draw some conclusions about further applications to teaching. A good monograph is Helen Driver, "Multiple Counselling: A Small Group Method for Personal Growth" (Madison: Monona Publications, 1954), in which a series of lesson plans for leaders of educational groups is provided. An effective "how to" approach to small groups in a variety of educational contexts is Herbert Thelen, **Dynamics of Groups at Work** (Chicago: The University of Chicago Press, 1954). Robert F. Hejna, **Speech Disorders and Nondirective Therapy** (New York: Ronald, 1960), discusses the use of various group methods applied to speech problems, particularly stuttering. A generally useful source with particular application to extension education is D. M. Hall, **Dynamics of Group Action** (Danville, Ill.: Interstate Printers and Publishers, 1957). A basic source in group therapy is S. R. Slavson, ed., **The Fields of Group Psychotherapy** (New York: International Universities Press, 1956). The book is a compendium of several approaches to therapy by noted authorities. The nondirective method is discussed briefly and clearly in Carl Rogers, "Techniques of a Helping Relationship," in Morris Stein, ed., **Contemporary Psychotherapies** (New York: The Free Press, 1961). For a Freudian approach to group therapy see Saul Scheidlinger, **Psychoanalysis and Group Behavior** (New York: Norton, 1952). A recent work that is quite clearly written and fairly complete is Abraham S. Luchins, **Group Therapy** (New York: Random House, 1964). Luchins surveys the various methods and applications of therapy, including semantitherapy and work therapy. Semantitherapy is also discussed in Harry Weinberg, **Levels of Knowing and Existence** (New York: Harper, 1958).

Most of the "formats" are considered in traditional discussion texts. Irving Lee, **Customs and Crises in Communication** (New York: Harper, 1954), offers a thorough discussion of the case method, with several samples for study. Randall Hoffman and Robert Plutchik, **Controversy** (New York: Putnam, 1959), provide some useful cases for classroom discussion, with commentary by the authors. Two good sources on role playing are Chris Argyris, **Roleplaying in Action** (Bulletin No. 16, New York State School of Industrial and Labor Relations, May, 1951), which treats the purposes and uses of role playing as well as techniques of motivation and evaluation; and Robert Blake, Raymond Corsini, and M. E. Shaw, **Roleplaying in Business and Industry** (New York: The Free Press, 1961), which describes roleplaying techniques for opening channels of communication.

An authoritative and highly sensitive work on communication techniques in small groups is Irving Lee, **How to Talk with People** (New York: Harper, 1952).

Chapter Four. A clear and comprehensive book based on standard agenda in group problem solving is Harold Zelko, **Successful Conference and Discussion Techniques** (New York: McGraw-Hill, 1957). In general, a truly excellent discussion of methods and techniques is Barnlund and Haiman, **Dynamics of Discussion** (Boston: Houghton

Mifflin, 1960). See especially the discussion of problem-solving on pages 71–98.

For those interested in learning PERT, the most effective device is a programmed learning series, **Planning and Scheduling with PERT and CPM** (Newburyport, Mass.: ENTELEK, Inc., 1964). This is a thorough and detailed program for mastering the computations in PERT, as well as the techniques for deriving insights into decision making from PERT information. Extensive bibliography on PERT in its various applications can be obtained from PERT Orientation and Training Center, **Bibliography: PERT and Other Management Systems and Techniques** (Washington, D.C.: Bolling Air Force Base, 1963). A simpler approach to PERT can be found in Federal Electric Corporation, **A Programmed Introduction to PERT** (New York: Wiley, 1963).

Evaluation of facts often poses a serious problem to small groups. Some good sources on evidence are Russel R. Windes and Arthur Hastings, **Argumentation and Advocacy** (New York: Random House, 1965), or Monroe Beardsley, **Thinking Straight** (Englewood Cliffs, Prentice-Hall, 1956). A good discussion of fallacious reasoning is W. Ward Fearnside and William B. Holther, **Fallacy** (Englewood Cliffs: Prentice-Hall, 1962). Refer also to a good general-semantics text like S. I. Hayakawa, **Language in Thought and Action,** 2d ed. (New York: Harcourt, Brace, 1964), for a discussion of the way in which one distinguishes fact, inference, and evaluation.

Chapter Five. Additional information about role taking as it affects hidden agenda can be found in Ralph H. Turner, "Role-taking, Role-standpoint, and Reference Group Behavior" (Indianapolis and New York: Bobbs-Merrill Reprint Series in the Social Sciences, No. 296), or George and Fanny Shaftel, **Role Playing: The Problem Story** (New York: National Council of Christians and Jews, 1952), which discusses the use of role playing to reveal hidden personality and emotional influences.

Games approaches to human interaction are thoroughly discussed in the books by Eric Berne: **Games People Play** (New York: Grove Press, 1964) and **Transactional Analysis in Psychotherapy** (New York: Grove Press, 1961).

Index